CHEF

BREAKFAST

My Turkish Summer

HOLLY WINTER HUPPERT

ALSO BY HOLLY WINTER HUPPERT

CHEESE FOR BREAKFAST

My Turkish Summer

Travel Safe!

♡ *Holly*

HOLLY WINTER HUPPERT

Winuply Press
Books for All

Edited by Betsy Osgood

Publisher's Cataloging-in-Publication data
Names: Huppert, Holly Winter, author.
Title: Cheese for breakfast: my Turkish summer. / Holly Winter Huppert.
Description: Lake Katrine [New York]: Winuply Press, 2020. Paperback.
Identifiers: ISBN 978-0-9983852-4-2
Subjects: LCSH: Turkey—Travel and description.
BISAC: TRAVEL / Essays & Travelogues. | BIOGRAPHY & AUTOBIOGRAPHY /
Personal Memoirs.
Classification: LCC DR429.4 | DDC 915–dc22

ISBN 978-0-9983852-4-2
Printed in the United States of America
First U.S. Edition
By Winuply Press: www.winuplypress.com

For the people of Turkey.
Thank you for sharing your beauty with me.

TABLE OF CONTENTS

PREFACE

After perusing the US government travel advisories for visiting Turkey, I watched a few videos, bought one travel guide and researched necessary precautions that would keep me safe as I prepared to travel to the country that is a part of both Europe and Asia.

Everything I read directed me to cover my head and wear long pants and long sleeves at all times, as the women there dress.

Got it.

As a kindergarten teacher, I have the summer off; travel it is.

I am a "Discovery Traveler," a term I think I made up; I like to show up in a new place and let thoughtful locals direct me. "Where should I go to hear music?" "What's the best place for *meze* (appetizers)?" "Where should I stay?"

I want to find out what life there is like away from the crowds of tourists and cruise-ship harbors. In fact if you tell me that X Cruise Ship Company docks in a particular city, likely I'll skip that city altogether. I don't care to duplicate the same adventure that others have taken.

Show me the back streets of Madrid where local children play stick ball in bare feet, or the beach parties on a remote Caribbean island where native men spend Father's Day cooking and pampering their families with gourmet barbecue fixings on the beach, and I feel like my travels are worth my time.

#1: thing I wanted to do in Turkey: Visit the Rumi museum and watch the monks whirl.

#2 thing I wanted to do in Turkey: Visit the ancient city of Ephesus.

#3 thing I wanted to do in Turkey: Write about everything.

Preferring to travel alone, I typically spend twelve hours each day out of the hotel room, exploring the city/town where I am and getting as far away from the tourist bubble as possible. At night when I'm back in my room, I'll write my stories and impressions from the day.

For me traveling is more like a job than a vacation.

I know how to travel safely. I never go out alone after dark, I get to know friendly locals at every stop who can direct me, and I never date on the road.

I know. The not-dating part surprises people. Traveling internationally and accepting dates is like playing a game where you don't know the rules: many men in other countries expect something from the date.

No, not sex. Marriage. Many other cultures think that just spending time together, even a few hours, proves compatibility. You can imagine that after I've turned down a man for whatever he expected or hoped for, his mood might change. Running from moody men in other countries where I don't speak the language isn't my idea of fun. But that's another story.

My friends Amy and Tim, full-time travelers (Gowithless.com), suggested I investigate a Work Away program where I could work in exchange for free room and board, as a way to spend time with locals. I paid the program's fee and started clicking. Many of the listings wanted someone to do the laundry, and/or the cleaning, the gardening, the shopping, and teach the children English while babysitting all day.

I wish I could tell you that this was an exaggeration.

After searching for hours, I found a listing by an archaeologist who was an expert on Ephesus, and his wife, an elementary school teacher. They had one 12-year-old daughter who wanted to learn English, and lived near Ephesus.

Seriously?

I wrote a message and with the help of a translation program that I would use every day of my trip, I translated my emails into Turkish, and the archaeologist wrote back, translating his words into English as we got to know each other.

After exchanging Facebook invitations and reading reviews from another traveler on the site, we decided my visit would be a good match for us all.

I bought a plane ticket and then heard back from the family that they changed their minds; they would not host me.

No worries. I'd start my travels in Izmir then head out to the beach at Çeşme. I booked hotels for the first days of the trip and started packing.

Days before my flight, a friend sent me a series of texts warning me that Turkey wasn't safe; her husband had read stories of women tourists detained at the airport.

Now? He tells me now?

I researched some more. There were articles about Turkish journalists being imprisoned and tourists who ended up in jail in Turkey for drugs, or buying antiquities and trying to smuggle them out of the country, or getting involved in black market dealings.

I texted my friend back, "When are the women jailed? At the beginning of their trip or at the end?"

"At the end."

I smiled and kept packing, thinking that if trouble would wait until the end of the trip, it was worth the risk.

The archaeologist's family had a change of heart; they sent me an email that my room was waiting for me.

"Are you sure?" I responded. "I will be in your area for one week."

I got an email back that said Turkey was waiting for me.

I accepted the invitation.

DAY 1: IZMIR: CUSTOMS

Changing planes in Istanbul's brand-new $12 billion airport (opened in April 2019) was a destination all its own. To get to the airport from the runway where the plane landed was a 20-minute ride in the plane.

Twenty minutes? That's a long taxi. I wanted to ask the pilots if we could fly to the terminal, as a time saver.

The airport had many Customs halls, each with different rules like a giant, international escape game. People in t-shirts that said "I speak English" directed. I guessed the "Visa" Customs hall was where I needed to line up, and a worker assured me I was in the right place. After a 10-minute wait, the Customs official sent me to the "Other Nationalities" Customs hall and then after waiting there for ten minutes, I was sent to "Domestic Departure" Customs hall.

When people complain about the long walks in this airport, they're not kidding. On my 90-minute layover, I waited for forty minutes and walked for forty-five minutes as fast as I could without ever circling back. Yes, I made my connection to Izmir.

At the Izmir airport, a kind woman pointed me to the bus that would drive me closer to my hotel. The driver slung my suitcase under, and I repeated to him several times, hoping that he would understand that I needed his help, "Swiss Efes Hotel." This swank hotel was only a five-minute walk to where I was staying.

The bus left the airport. My first views of Izmir were: at first ugly, then green, then European wonder. Fashionable people walked along busy streets. Almost half of the women had their heads covered and were wearing long sleeves and long pants.

Turkey.

I watched for a sign that this place I was in was far different than the place I left. More than the people who walked the streets, the billboards told the story of a new place. Women in the billboards wore head scarves and were more modestly dressed than even the women walking along the sidewalks.

Hello, Turkey.

The bus stopped and many people got off. The driver walked back and pointed to me.

"Swiss Efes Hotel?" I asked.

He pointed out the front of the bus window to the hotel.

I collected my suitcase from him, and he wouldn't drive away unless I walked towards the hotel. To appease him I walked towards the Swiss Efes, then turned towards my more affordable hotel, which was in the opposite direction, the moment the bus was out of sight.

My hotel, the family-run Piano Hotel (there's no piano on the premises and no piano music playing, so I referred to it as the "No Piano Hotel"), greeted me with a warm welcome and an upgrade.

I had a small room with a bathroom and a shower and an air conditioner. I wasn't sure if this was the best hotel room I've ever been in because I was so tired or because I kept my expectations low so I wouldn't be disappointed.

I found my way to the port in Izmir and wandered for hours, too tired to eat dinner or figure out why different elderly women approached and whispered to me in Turkish, as if each were offering help of some kind. Some black-market shenanigans? A travel tip? The recipe for gluten-free baklava? I responded with a "no" and a shrug and walked away.

Actually I wasn't too tired to eat, but I was too tired to go through the ordeal to get food. I would have to ask for gluten-free food and then show them the piece of paper that was folded up in my purse that explained celiac disease in Turkish: I could not eat bread, I could not eat anything made with wheat flour.

The list goes on; it would take a great deal of energy to figure out which foods I could eat without getting sick. I wasn't in the mood to work that hard tonight.

I had some almonds in my suitcase, almonds for dinner.

The time was seven hours ahead of New York. I felt like I was living in the future.

Upstairs in the Hisar Mosque.

Women buying scarves at the Kemeralti Market in Izmir. Holly Winter
Huppert bought the scarf with zigzags.

DAY 2: IZMIR: MOSQUE

B reakfast at my hotel included boiled eggs, raw vegetables, veggies cooked in oils, six kinds of cheese, olives, spiced potatoes, yogurt, breakfast drinks (and breads which I couldn't eat), and lots of local olive oil, for no extra charge.

Cheese for breakfast? A big win.

I wandered along the Kordon and watched as the ferry boats arrived with stylish people heading to work. There are many stray dogs and cats sitting in the shade cooling off in the morning breeze. Who takes care of them? Is there water for them to drink? Where do they go when the pavement gets hot?

I headed to the Hisar Mosque, which dates back to 1597 and is the largest mosque in the city. Men sat at special faucets to wash their feet before they prayed. I wasn't sure what to do, so I didn't wash, but took off my shoes and covered my head. (My shoulders and knees were already covered.) This was my first mosque. It had a domed ceiling and simple blue and gold motifs and a lot of twinkling lights.

There were many men praying downstairs; I proceeded upstairs to see what it was like and discovered that this is where the women pray. I read my guidebook this morning to learn about mosques; it failed to mention that women pray upstairs. (Written by men?) I kneeled and then sat on my legs, like the other women, closed my eyes and meditated.

As women entered, they gave my shoulder a squeeze as they walked past. I thought it was a touch of solidarity, but I wasn't sure. They didn't greet each other in any way. The other women finished praying and left, and for a moment I was alone and wept slow tears of gratitude for being in such a beautiful place. I am so fortunate to have the time to travel.

I spent hours wandering through the Kemeralti Market which is a labyrinthine bazaar from the seventeenth century. Many, many Turkish people shop here. (I haven't heard a word of English spoken yet, unless it was a Turkish person talking to me.) Tarps cover the entire area, so it was a cool respite from the 93-degree sun. Though I promised myself that I wouldn't buy anything, I couldn't resist.

A group of women surrounded a man selling scarves for 5 TL (Turkish lira), which is less than a dollar. I watched for a while and was relieved that there was no haggling; I bought one. I also bought a beautiful leather journal for 35 TL (just over $4) and spent the rest of the day hugging it. A new journal!

I took a break back at my hotel to drink water and cool down, which is a challenge for me: I don't like to stop. Next, I walked to the pedestrian street, Kibris Şehitleri Caddesi, in Alsancak. Bustling. Stylish. Party. That tink-tink-tink sound as people stir sugar cubes into their tea. I wasn't hungry for dinner, so I walked and watched.

I walked home along the Kordon to see if the fishermen were catching anything and saw a homeless man cuddling a stray dog. I couldn't tell who was happier, the man, the dog or me.

A woman walks along the Kordon in Izmir.

A tulip-shaped teacup holds 1/4 cup of liquid and is served
with a small bowl. The cup is smaller than a pen.

DAY 3: IZMIR: RING

Izmir is 7,800 years old and has been in a never-ending game of "hot potato" for its entire life. This seaport has been ruled by the Lydians, the Romans, the Persians, the Ottomans, the Ionians, the Muppets and others. (Cut the Muppets from that list.)

Not to be a name dropper, but Marcus Aurelius hung out here and so did Socrates. I was looking forward to going to the Izmir Archaeological Museum, which is filled with relics found—right here.

I wondered if the people of Izmir dug up statues in their flower gardens. Best garden decorations, ever! A headless marble statue would be better than a typical scarecrow.

The GPS on my phone directed me through new neighborhoods. I enjoyed looking in the windows of the shops along the way as I did my best to ignore the stray dogs and cats that followed me in hopes of a treat.

The museum organized its collections by age; I tried to understand the different periods and listened to the audio guide again and again. Even though the guide was in English, I walked away with one main learning: they found a statue of a priest and he was wearing a ring.

I hung out in the Kültürpark so I could remember what trees

looked like, and then walked over to Luna Park and checked out the rides.

I was bummed that this is my last night in Izmir. To celebrate my birthday (Hello 54!), I treated myself to a giant bowl of ice cream and sat on a bench near the ocean and watched people walk by.

Life is sweet.

Arriving at the Çiftlik Butik Otel, an oasis in travel.

The view of the pool and the ocean from Holly Winter Huppert's room.

DAY 4: ÇEŞME: BLUE

When the bus headed down the highway before I paid for my ticket or double-checked that I was on the right bus, I worried that my last driver put me on the wrong bus. What if I pronounced Çeşme (chess-may) so badly that I was being driven to a different place? (Like Chechnya, Russia.) The bus was half-filled with people, including two British women sitting behind me who giggled over their dating practices and a Turkish couple in the seats in front of me who might have been joining a—travel club.

As the bus passed apartment blocks that lined both sides of the road, a man stood, collected bus fares and handed out tickets. What a relief: I started breathing again. I pulled up Çeşme on my phone and showed him. He pointed to the price on the ticket, 30 TL (less than $4).

Hopefully, I could figure out when to get off. He smiled at the couple sitting in front of me and said something that might have been the equivalent of "Get a room," and they smiled and toned it down.

The bus stopped. I said to the driver, "Çeşme?" And pointed to the ground. He nodded and I thought that one day I would buy the town a welcome sign.

I finally got an address for the hotel late last night, why was it so hard to get? I Googled it this morning. My hotel was an 85-minute walk from the center of town. Seriously? The guidebooks said you didn't need a car here; wrong again. The taxi driver's eyes got big when he looked at the address, making me think we needed to pack a picnic for the ride. I rubbed my fingers together for the universal "How much?" sign.

Forty TL ($5), more than the bus.

I suffered hotel envy as we passed bright hotels on the beach and big hotels next to restaurants. The entire town reeked of chaos: people walking, cars beeping, yachts crawling with people in expensive bathing suits. This was not the sleepy resort town I had read about.

We drove along the Aegean coast; the water was calm. What color was that water? Blue, what? All I could come up with was blue blue. After twenty minutes, we turned off the main road away from the ocean and drove up a hill filled with scrub brush. I tensed; the property had boasted an ocean view. Liars!

The driveway was over a mile long. Oh? We arrived at a villa surrounded by wilderness and covered with lush red flowers. Beautiful. How many acres do they have? There's room to breathe here.

The manager met me with a smile and held my passport in his hands while he slowly said, "America. America," as if he had just learned that it was a real place. I had to help him find my passport number.

My spacious room opened to the pool and had an ocean view. I sat in a chair, absorbing the beauty around me. This. This.

As far as I could tell, there were four guest rooms total. I was the only one who spoke English. It felt like I was a guest in someone's house, so I unpacked.

They made me dinner and I swam in the pool (they mopped behind me when I got out). I nestled into peace. I may never go to town. I might live here forever.

I love when things are better than expected.

A walk in the wilderness.

A deserted house with bars on the windows.

DAY 5: ÇEŞME: JAIL?

At 6:00 AM I walked down the hill towards the Aegean; I love to take before-breakfast walks. I found the ocean and was reminded that not all coastline has a beach. I wanted to walk on a beach.

I'd dressed in long shorts and a sleeveless shirt because this was a beach area, only to find the other women walking had all limbs covered and their heads wrapped. Why was it so hard for me to get the dress code right?

Rather than walking on a sidewalk, I checked the map then doubled back past my hotel: there was a beach with sand a ten-minute walk in the other direction. I walked quickly along dusty roads, enjoying the desolate landscape; this was a different kind of beauty. I walked past tomato farms and small cinder-block houses with large rocks holding the metal roofs on.

I reached the top of the ridge where I could see the water and checked the time. How could I have nine minutes left to walk? I checked my map settings. Car. My map settings were set to car; when I changed the setting to walking, I had another forty minutes to go. Sigh.

I didn't have enough water to walk all that way. As far as I could see there were no stores or restaurants to buy a drink near the ocean.

I turned back and let my GPS guide me along a different route to the left that would be two minutes faster to return to my hotel. Faster would be better; I was running low on water. There were old rock walls along this dirt road and intensely thorny bushes. It's endlessly exciting to be in a place that is different from any place I've been before.

I took a photo of the stone wall. I took an artsy photo of the thorn bushes. Oh, look. A cinder-block house. It looked abandoned, but you never know. I made a video to show how there was nothing around the house, and at the end I stopped and stared. My eyes kept going back to the windows. Why? What was it about the windows?

Bars. The windows all had bars on them.

I stared. Why would a house way out here have bars on the windows? Goosebumps grew on my arms and legs as if my body knew something my mind hadn't figured out yet. Raising chickens, I thought. That's just a big barn. The bars are so the chickens can't escape. My goosebumps grew and I shivered as if I'd caught a little chill. No, the roof was terracotta, better than the other shacks I'd passed; this wasn't a barn.

Jail. It really looked like a jail. Way out here. Maybe someone was in there. I desperately wanted to go inside and check. Maybe someone in there needed water. What if it were a holding cell for young girls who were trafficked? What if? What if? I stood staring. I should go in.

But I couldn't. I walked away slowly. I didn't understand trespassing laws in Turkey, which is why I didn't help myself to a ripe tomato from the farms I'd walked past. I really wanted a tomato, but I wouldn't cross the line.

I couldn't go in the building that looked like a jail. I had to walk away. I walked slowly at first, then faster. Nobody else was walking out there. I walked faster. There was no traffic out here; not one car had passed by. I tried to tune in to the nature around me, but my rose-colored glasses had darkened.

I made it back to the hotel by 7:30, a little sunburned and dehydrated from my early morning walk. The 18-year-old worker, who seemed to work all hours of the day and night, saw me come in. He stood, staring, as if thinking that I didn't sleep in my bed last night.

There was no way to explain, so I smiled and said, "*Merhaba*" (Hello) and stepped into my room. I turned on the air conditioning and lay on my bed for hours.

I was famished and looked for breakfast but couldn't find the buffet. I watched as a young couple sat at a table. Nope, no food for them, either. A few minutes later I peeked out again and their table was filled with food, like a gift from a genie. It can be a challenge when you don't know the rules. I sat at a table next to the olive trees and after about ten minutes, breakfast arrived.

An omelet. Cream with honey. Cheese with blackberry jam. Apricot jam. Cherry jam. Cucumbers and peppers. Sliced tomatoes, yogurt and four kinds of cheese.

The Turkish have a saying, "Eat sweet. Speak sweetly." So I ate the cherries out of the jam before I tackled the eggs. Yes, I ate sweetly.

Later I walked into town wearing my Russian peasant outfit that kept my arms and legs mostly covered, as the guidebooks recommend, and found that the yacht crowd wore expensive clothes boasting lots of skin. Really? I ordered a *kahve* (coffee) at a café before I realized they were playing old American songs. "Stayin' Alive" was followed by the song, "Killing Me Softly." Yes, the universe has a sense of humor.

I took a taxi back to the hotel, where they played Turkish music as the sun set. It was a perfect sunset.

DAY 6: ÇIFTLIK: HYDRATE

I looked up the symptoms of heat exhaustion, and like a greedy tourist, I had them all. When had I stopped sweating? I kicked the stray dogs out of the shade where I was walking in town and sipped water while the breeze cooled me. The first rule of travel is hydrate; I needed to double my water intake to make up for the high temperatures.

The internet mentioned that if you have every one of the symptoms of heat exhaustion and you're confused, you need to go to the hospital. Um, not the travel excitement I was looking for. I figured that if the hospital could slowly add two liters of liquid into my body, I could, too.

Time to hydrate. I returned to the hotel and sipped water for hours. By one o'clock the nausea stopped and so did the confusion, but the crowning achievement was that I was once again covered in sweat.

The shade of the pool was my afternoon refuge; I used up my second pen writing in my journal since my keyboard died. Miss that keyboard. It was time for more adventure, so I walked down the hill and turned right at the sea. That's where I found my people. Regular People. Locals. There was no champagne-sipping or snapping fingers at the wait staff from the back of a yacht. In fact I didn't see any yachts in Çiftlik.

I sat in a café and made small talk with a Turkish woman who probably shared my decade. I spoke in English, she in Turkish. She showed me her ripped shopping bag and discussed what was most likely her tough-day stories. I talked about heat exhaustion and feeling relaxed for the first time since school let out. For twenty minutes we spoke back and forth, taking turns in a language the other didn't understand.

Then she looked at her watch, paid for our drinks, gave me a quick hug and said, "Good-bee, a-fr-nd!!" It was a shock to hear her speak English.

To return the thoughtfulness, I said my Turkish word of the day back to her, "*Salatalik!*" (Cucumber)

She shook my hand and we both laughed one more time.

A stray cat naps in the shade next to the castle in Çeşme.

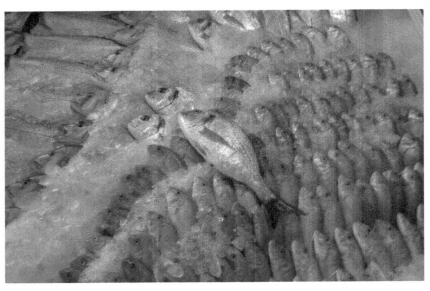

Fresh caught fish caught mere yards from the Canbaba restaurant in
Çiftlik.

DAY 7: ÇIFTLIK: FISH FOR DINNER

The manager of the hotel caught me sneaking down the hotel's driveway to go to town. He stopped me and insisted on driving me wherever I wanted to go. I typed into Google Translate so he could read it in Turkish, "I don't need a ride. I am going to Çiftlik, only a ten-minute walk."

He insisted on driving. We got to town and he asked where I wanted to eat. I typed the word "fish" into the translator. He made me memorize the name of a restaurant. Canbaba. He spoke into his translation app and explained to me that it was the best fish on the whole peninsula.

Mostly I've been eating inexpensive kebabs because I love lamb and kebabs are gluten-free. Not tonight.

I found the restaurant and noted the white linen tablecloths. This was not going to be a cheap meal. I chose a table with a sea view in the shade because the sun was hot even at 7:00 PM. There were six waiters staring at me. I was confused, was I supposed to choose my waiter?

I waited. They waited.

I smiled and said hello in English and then in Turkish. They smiled and nodded, and one waiter stepped forward.

"Do you want fish for dinner?" the only English-speaking waiter asked.

I nodded and showed him my gluten-free information sheet that always gets a murmur of appreciation for being written in Turkish. He walked me into the kitchen where the manager, who had studied in London, took over in a perfect British accent.

He showed me the starters, twenty-five different dishes, and suggested I order several. I got the broccoli, the seaweed with garlic sauce and the beets. I motioned that this was enough food.

"You are getting fat in your stomach," he said, agreeing with me.

I smiled. Either he'd been stalking me on the internet and noticed a weight gain, or he didn't fully grasp the future tense. I think the latter but am open to the former.

They opened the fish case and waited for my approval.

"It was caught eight hundred meters from here this afternoon," the manager said. I chose a small fish and was sent back to my table.

This was going to be an expensive meal. No menus. No prices. A hundred dollars, I hoped. Not more than a hundred with a tip. If this place catered to the yacht crowd, it could be more.

I squeezed some lemon into my glass while all six waiters watched. One rushed forward to fill my glass with water from the 1.5 liter bottle they had placed on my table. I thanked him and sipped my drink while all six waiters continued to watch me. Were they ignoring the other five tables? It's a good thing that as a teacher I am used to being stared at.

A man, impeccably dressed in white linen that almost matched the tablecloths, approached my table with the air of someone very important, and said something in Turkish. A waiter whispered something, and the man said in English, "I am John Baba."

I smiled, wondering if he were a movie star or something. I shook his hand and murmured pleasantries and after he walked away, I realized his last name was part of the restaurant's name, Canbaba. He must be the owner. I wondered if he knew the meaning of "can" in English?

The mezes were amazing, I could eat that seaweed every day. The fish was cooked perfectly, and they drizzled fresh olive oil from the region over it, which was so good that I debated chugging more oil directly from the bottle. I couldn't swig the oil, because those six waiters who were still watching me would be confused.

"I'm finished," I said to my waiter after I had taken as long as possible to eat. My dishes were cleared from the table. I admired the setting sun while I waited for the check that never arrived.

Twenty minutes later I said to my waiter, "I'm done." He nodded and walked away.

Another twenty minutes passed, and I said to a busboy, "Check?" The team rushed to get my waiter. He handed me the check and I handed it back with my credit card. No reason to look, I wasn't going to debate the price

The price of this fine dining experience? One hundred fifty TL, or $26.56. Really. Turkey is so cheap right now. I left a big tip sticking out from my water glass and later remembered that you must hand the tip directly to the waiter, or the owner gets to keep it. Darn it. There's so much to remember when visiting another culture.

Before I walked out, my waiter shook my hand and said, "See you tomorrow."

I thanked him for taking such good care of me and before I left I shook hands with every waiter and busboy, and they all smiled the biggest smiles. Thanks, guidebook, you got that one right, shake hands with everyone in the group.

But this was my last night on the peninsula so I wouldn't return the next day. The restaurant manager met me at the door and said, "You made a mistake, you should have saved this paradise for the end of your trip. Now Turkey will be sad for you."

"It's okay," I said. "I want to see all of the faces of Turkey."

Boats in Çiftlik in the early morning.

Holly Winter Huppert wanted to know if the antique dial phone at the Çiftlik Butik Otel worked, or if it was just for show. It worked and it was for show, too.

DAY 8: SELÇUK: LAYERS

I took one last walk by the Aegean for my early morning stroll and got there before the fishermen left for the day, and just in time for a major dog fight. Strays ran past me to join the brutality, like a gang fight where you jump into the fray just because if one fights, we all fight. Barking, biting, tackling. The locals walked by without so much as a glance, as if this were so typical it didn't warrant a look.

I thought about an article I'd read that dubbed the stray dogs and cats of Turkey "wild" and kept to the other side of the street. I couldn't peg what started the fight: there was no pile of food they were arguing over and no apparent territory invasion. After several minutes, the dogs stopped their rude behavior as if on cue, and returned to innocently sniffing each other and scrounging the beach for food.

The village bread had just been delivered to the bakery in crates stacked on top of each other on the sidewalk; I may not be able to eat bread, but the smell was a reward in itself: sweet, savory, doughy. As I walked back to my hotel, motorbikes sped past with bags of bread bouncing from the drivers' hands.

How come the stray dogs don't steal the fresh loaves of bread?

The manager of the hotel offered to drive me to the bus; I

accepted. He turned up the Turkish music and let me look out the window. After a while I used my phone to translate questions.

He and his wife were from Bulgaria, and he suggested I travel to meet them there next year when they are home. I accepted his offer with a smile of gratitude, as I always accept every travel offer whether or not it is practical at the time; you never know...

He parked on a sidewalk and walked me to the bus parking lot. There were buses pointed in every direction, like a giant bus compass. The manager asked a driver where my bus was, the driver shouted his answer at me as if I could understand louder Turkish. Yeah, yeah Mr. Impatient Turkish Man, don't worry, there's always someone else to help me find my way.

The manager asked someone else and loaded my suitcase onto the Izmir airport bus that would take me to a transfer station so I could head into the city. I thanked the manager, again, for his help and then we kissed goodbye, first on one cheek, then on the other.

It was time for me to meet the family I would stay with for a week.

I met the father, an archaeologist, at his archaeology museum in Izmir. He was around 40 years old with short, dark hair. He wore a short-sleeved shirt tucked into long pants. He had a quick smile and I could tell that his staff liked him.

They all stared at me. I worried that they worried about inviting a strange woman into their home. The archaeologist invited me into his office, which was roughly the size of my house back home, and offered me tea. In broken English, he told me how he coordinates five different museums and then asked me about my job.

I told everyone, via the translation program, that I was a teacher and a writer and that this was my first time in Turkey.

We found our way to the train station and after he paid for my ticket, we rode the train together for the hour-and-a-half trip to his small city. He used the translation program and asked if I had any questions about my visit to his archaeological museum on a day he was away.

I asked him if children find artifacts every time they go outside to play in their yards.

He laughed for a long time, then took out Google Translate and showed me the word, "Layers."

I told him how as children we would find arrowheads from the natives of long ago, or little knives in the dirt in upstate New York, and how we would collect them.

He shook his head slowly, *imagine little children playing with swords*, but the topic moved on before I could explain.

He was discussing the 8,000-year history of Izmir and insisted that my country didn't start in 1776. I had to be the one to tell him that when the white men claimed America, they erased all prior civilizations; the USA was considered the first country of my land.

"I don't understand," he wrote in the translate app. "The native people aren't on your calendar?"

His wife and daughter were waiting for us. The wife had a fast smile and dark curly hair. She was at once fashionable and down to earth, wearing a short skirt and tank top. Their daughter had long straight hair, and wore a tank top and shorter shorts with words written in English.

They showed me to my bedroom, a long, narrow room with a twin bed at the far end under a window. There was a desk and chair where I could write and a sofa where I could unpack.

The daughter said shyly, "We eat dinner now."

I could tell that she'd practiced that line and I nodded at being ready for dinner and at her perfect English sentence.

They lived on the third floor of a modern apartment building. It had a small kitchen with a balcony and two other bedrooms. I was relieved to see that there was a regular toilet; I'd been worried that I'd have to use a squat toilet for the whole week.

They made an amazing lamb dinner and I was feeling pretty good for being treated like a queen. They made dinner for me! They set the table for me! We ate and used technology to communicate.

The mother was a first-grade teacher and the daughter played piano and volleyball, but not at the same time. We sat at the table after dinner getting to know each other. The mother's classroom had no picture books; she ate lunch with her students and got no planning periods all day.

I spoke into the translation program, "You get no breaks during the school day?"

"Five minutes to use the bathroom between subjects," she answered.

After dinner, the daughter let me know that she loves Katy Perry, so we watched Katy Perry videos on the internet while we both sang along.

A family friend, an English teacher, and her daughter with long hair visited. The English teacher practiced her near-perfect English. "America?" she said. "Where were you born?"

"New York."

She asked, "Where do you live now?"

"New York."

She said it was unusual to get a real American to visit Selçuk, which I took as a compliment, thinking they must get a lot of fake Americans.

She told the story of her uncle coming to visit from America and being told to wear long sleeves and long pants on his trip. She said he was most uncomfortable on the hot days. They had to lend him better clothes. She added that Turkey doesn't have a dress code.

She wore shorts and a tank top, so did her daughter, and so did the family I was staying with. Every guidebook and website I looked at warned that I needed to dress conservatively by covering up.

"How long ago did your uncle visit?" I asked as I sat sweltering in my long-sleeved shirt and long pants.

"Twenty years ago."

Yeah? Well, nothing's changed.

Breakfast picnic at Yoncaköy Beach, near Selçuk.

The family Holly Winter Huppert stayed with in Selçuk and on the left is
the daughter's friend with the long hair.

The daughter of the family Holly Winter Huppert stayed with sits at a cafe in Selçuk.

A picnic with friends at the park. (From the left: English teacher, archaeologist, mother, English teacher's husband, the friend with the long hair and the daughter of the family.)

DAY 9: SELÇUK: PICNIC

Y oncaköy Beach is about twenty minutes away and has sand along one edge and jagged cliffs along another. It was worth the effort for the mother, the daughter, the daughter's long-haired friend and I to carry chairs, a card table and all of our things up the cliff to a flat part and set up for our breakfast picnic packed by the mother. We were so overheated from the climb that we left our shoes at the steps and climbed into the cold water to swim with little fishes.

I swam to the cove in the cliffs. This area is 8,000 years old; I wanted to find something to prove it, but there wasn't a shovel in sight, so I swam around and dreamed of who might have hung out along those cliffs years ago.

My new word of the day is cheese, *"peynir."* (Sounds like "painish," rhymes with Danish.)

There's something about the freshness of the food in Turkey that's making me feel like my taste buds have found an "on" switch that I didn't know was off. I asked what kind of cheese we were eating for breakfast, and the answer was given with a shrug and the tapping of the translation program, "sheep's cheese."

No brand name or color of the wrapper was offered, just that it was something from the market. The cheese was soft, tart and creamy and made everything else taste better; I didn't know cheese could have that kind of power. And I now know what a cherry is supposed to taste like, and so starts my cherry kick.

The daughter and her friend had to go to a volleyball game, so the mother and I stopped for ice cream from a place that put our scoops in glass dishes with small, flat-ended spoons. For the mother's first English lesson with me, she picked the phrase, "I need to..." and we paired as many scenarios as we could think of: "I need to eat ice cream." Her friend came along and joined the lesson.

"What can you already say?" I asked him.

He said, "What is your name? Where do you live? Do you like the color red?"

We practiced the phrase-of-the-day and he said, "I need to smoke a cigarette," which confused me for reasons of health; I don't normally compliment someone for smoking a cigarette, but his sentence was perfect.

Later the 12-year-old daughter and her long-haired friend were ready for their English lessons. They have mastered a lot of vocabulary but didn't know how to apply it, so I asked as many higher-level questions as I could about King Arthur before we started reading about him. "How do we know about King Arthur?" I asked. "Did he star in television or movies or YouTube videos?"

The girls were unsure. One asked, "Is this question a very trick?"

The mother and I have a lot common. She wears the same clothing style that is hanging in my closet at home. We eat the same kinds of foods, albeit at different times of day. I wouldn't think of eating cheese and olives for breakfast at home, but I was getting used to it.

She asked me if I wanted to use her organic coconut oil, and I showed her that I had the same exact jar that I'd bought a few days before. We both stood at the bathroom mirror, adding oil on our dry elbows, and I shared my secret oil concoction that I made at home and carried with me to oil our faces.

"Now we go!" she said.

We piled into the car and a song played on the radio in English, "You're Just too Good to be True." I sang along.

The family and the daughter's long-haired friend and I were

heading up to the mountains to hang out in an old village and watch the sunset, but the moment we arrived, the red ball of a sun fell behind the mountains. Darn it, missed the sunset.

We walked through the Math Village that hosted a summer program for high school students. There were kids playing ping-pong and other kids sitting together and laughing and eating popcorn—no chaperones in sight.

The daughter looked around and said to me, "Next year I want to come here to study math."

"Me too," I said.

We checked out a museum in Şirince Village and the mother pointed out a kindergarten diploma that was written in Arabic during the Ottoman Empire's rule in 1931. The official language of Turkey has changed so many times over the years, imagine trying to keep up as you write report cards.

As we walked around the village, cars passed us spraying road-dust over our group. The mother looked at me and pantomimed putting oil on her face and arms, then getting covered in grit. We laughed.

"I need to shower," she said, and we laughed again.

And so ended another perfect day.

DAY 10: SELÇUK: STRAY

The mother of the family I'm staying with handed me a piece of frozen aloe when I walked into the kitchen. She demonstrated what to do with it by rubbing her piece on her face, arms and hands. I lifted the frozen plant to my face; it felt like I was peeling away a layer of skin. I copied her through my discomfort, covering all exposed skin with the frozen piece of plant, because as any woman knows, when it comes to beauty regimens, we love trying new things.

Within moments my skin felt awake and refreshed. I stood dripping with aloe and asked her what I should do next. She shrugged her shoulders, not understanding.

"Should I leave the aloe dripping?" I asked her as I pointed to aloe dripping off my chin. She shrugged again, still not understanding. I walked into the bathroom and pointed to the water then to my face.

She said, "I need to you wash with the water."

And so started our ability to graduate from the translation program for small talk.

I rinsed off the goo and told her my skin never felt so soft or hydrated.

"Good?" she asked, not understanding.

"Very good," I said.

"Very good," she repeated with a dreamy look on her face, the look she makes when she's trying to memorize new English words.

It became a game to have me try foods or experiences that were new to me. Today for breakfast we had little spoons filled with rose jam.

"Rose?" I asked. "Like the flower?"

"Yes," the daughter said, "like the flower."

I ate it and became an instant fan; the petals added texture to the sweetness. They also had me try tomato jam. I said, "I prefer the rose jam," and pointed to the bottle.

"Sad," the mother said. "I like flower good, too. You like tomato?"

We laughed at her joke of not wanting to share the rose jam and then we both dripped more rose jam onto our spoons. I was quite pleased that my new habit of eating jam by the spoonful was alive and well and culturally acceptable in this family.

For the daughter's English lesson, I found an online copy of *Green Eggs and Ham*, the Dr. Seuss children's picture book. The family had never heard of this book or this author and it was an honor to share it with them.

The daughter was able to read the words flawlessly and even understood it with her years of English practice, but found the repeating phrases were like tongue twisters. The book did not convince her to try green eggs and ham.

She said, "I think green is bad color for eggs."

I asked a lot of questions about the stray animals.

The mother asked me, "You have street dog cat with New York?"

I held up my fingers to show a small amount and said, "A little."

The mother picked up the translate program. "Why is this so upsetting to you?"

I took her phone and said, "In my country cats and dogs beg at the table even when they are inside the house and getting enough food. Here the dogs and cats do not bother us in the restaurant."

The mother took the phone back. "People who like cats and dogs feed the street dogs. They are not hungry."

I said, "In my country cats and dogs jump on the table to eat extra food. And they shred open garbage bags to find more food even if they are not hungry."

It's almost like there's some invisible animal trainer that teaches the strays to not go after the bread crates that are stacked outside restaurants in the early morning, or dig through the bags of garbage that are waiting for collection. The strays don't approach strangers for food or attention or jump on tables. How could this be?

As our day continued, Daughter pointed out pots of water around Selçuk. "For the animals."

We walked past a restaurant and some cats were eating a pile of something on the ground. "Is that fish?" I asked my friends.

"Fish restaurant." The mother pointed to the picture of a fish on the restaurant sign as the cats gnawed on fish bones without any hissing or arguing of any kind between them, as if there were a sharing code in place, even for strays.

"What about the doctor?" I asked. "Who takes the animals to the doctor?"

The daughter said, "People who love animals take to doctor."

I nodded. Sometimes I understand the words but have more questions than I can formulate. That's why I wanted to stay with a family, so they might help explain their culture to me and so I could experience their lives at a family level, not at the tourist level.

We met some of the mother's friends at the Ephesus Museum, an enormous building that is filled with artifacts that date back many thousands of years and come from this one archaeological site. That's why I wanted to come to Selçuk so badly, to see the ancient city of Ephesus, where these artifacts came from.

The daughter and her long-haired friend proudly taught me the lessons of the various empires that built, tore down, relocated and exploited the famous archaeological site. The girls would call out, "interesting learning now" in the museum whenever they thought my mind was wandering from their astute teachings.

I couldn't imagine having to memorize the history of 8,000 years of occupation for my country; the girls seemed to understand each occupation and the gifts it left behind. It was possible that the complicated history of their country made them natural historians, compared to the 6th grade students from home who knew that Betsy Ross sewed our flag, but little else.

The mother taught us the "Rabbit Game," which is based on the fondness for rabbits of Eros, the Greek god of love, when he was a child. Our group laughed so loudly that the people who thought a museum should be a place of quiet contemplation were insulted and left, which I thought was perfect. Because without those stuffy types around, I found the courage to ask the mother if I could stand behind a headless statue to get my picture taken. (I was once thrown out of the Metropolitan Museum of Art in New York City for getting a friend to pose for a picture in this same way.)

The women in my group squinted at me; I'd gone too far. Breaking a rule. Posing with a relic. Treating serious artifacts as folly. Acting like a tourist and not a friend. I was about to apologize and ask the girls for some more interesting learnings, when Mother looked around and said, "Okay. No touch statue."

Classic tourist photo taken, check.

They each lined up to have their photo taken with the headless statue, too, and I worried that perhaps I was a bad influence.

Later I taught the daughter a piano lesson to learn the song, "If the Stars were Mine." Which would scare my former piano teacher; my piano skills are minimal. "I love this song," Daughter said, and practiced it again and again, first one hand, then two, while we sang along to the lyrics I'd printed out for her.

When her father got home at 7:30 PM, he suggested that we rush to the beach to watch the sunset, but we'd have to leave right away. We grabbed some snacks and our cameras, and he drove.

"Maybe tonight we will see the sun," I joked, since last night the ball of fire had set moments before we arrived.

"We will like sun today," the father prophesied.

But as we drove closer, the sun sank closer and closer to the horizon.

When we arrived, we grabbed the chairs and the table from the trunk of the car and dropped them on the beach as we ran to the edge of the ocean.

"Stop," the daughter yelled at the sun. "We want to see you up."

We laughed and ran faster, which is difficult to do on a sandy beach.

"Now. Fast," the father said. "Take a picture of sun in sky."

We laughed and snapped photos of a sliver of sun sitting on the horizon.

"More picture," the father said. "You remember we find sun this day."

We sat in our chairs and ate peanuts that were grown in Turkey and local cherries; since the family had figured out my love of local cherries, there are always cherries for us to share. The wind off the water felt colder than the posted temperature, so after an hour or so we left and met the English teacher and her husband at a café in town for a cup of something warm.

We settled outside with our warm drinks, and one friend asked about the museum and if I'd had a good time.

Before I could answer, my friends were shouting my name, urgently, which confused me; we were sitting at the table together, why were they shouting?

"Now."

"Holly, like."

I tried to piece together the last string of conversation with this new outburst. It can be tough speaking to people who are learning my language.

"This," the father shouted urgently. "Now. This."

I looked at them, shaking my head, not understanding, then noticed they all had their hands over their teacups.

"Now," the mother said. "I need to."

I put my hand over my teacup just as a truck drove by spraying a liquid into the air and all over all of us. A mist lifted off the spray and covered us and the trees around us with a layer of...something.

I looked at my friends.

"Insect," the father said.

"That was insect spray, pesticide?" I asked.

"Yes," they all said, keeping their hands over their cups until the mist settled.

I wanted a shower and a new set of clothes, and would it be too much to get a new cup of tea? Since I didn't cover my lumps of sugar, I wouldn't eat them. And though it is likely that I just got a city-size dose of Roundup, none of my fingers fell off, which was fortunate.

If I were comparing new experiences, I'd prefer the rose jam.

The English teacher's husband asked, "What breakfast you eat New York?"

I said, "Never cheese. Or olives. Or tomatoes. Or cucumber."

The friends were quiet.

The father said, "If olives no breakfast, when?"

"Lunch or dinner," I said. "In salads, or with meat. Or as a snack."

The English teacher's husband said, "It is no breakfast no cheese."

I nodded in agreement.

I told them I posted a picture of the breakfast foods of Turkey, and that my friends back home were surprised that we ate cheese and olives and vegetables for breakfast.

The group of friends laughed around the table.

The father said, "Maybe new summer we all us go at New York and breakfast cheese, olives with people of you."

"Yes! Please come," I said. "I have some jams for you to try."

Shopping for cheese with the archaeologist at the outdoor market.

Wearing headscarves in a mosque. (From the left: the English teacher, her daughter—the girl with the long hair, and the daughter of the family.)

DAY 11 A: SELÇUK: DIFFERENCES

It was a big responsibility being the most recent cultural representative of the United States that my friends in Turkey had spent time with. The family noticed the things I paid attention to, and I worried that they would generalize my impressions as the way of all Americans.

A vine-ripened tomato made me stare; they were everywhere, these red pyramids that boasted the reddest red and the sweetest sweet, as if they were tomato candy in disguise. At home it was rare to find a truly ripened tomato for sale, so when I saw one it registered as an oddity.

"Look at that tomato!" I'd say to my friends as they looked at each other slowly, as if registering that Americans are tomato deprived.

I stopped to photograph stray cats, bread vendors and every meal they prepared. I loved visiting a place where so many things were the same, but different.

When I first arrived at their apartment and was getting the tour, I looked out of the kitchen's balcony and saw that workers were replacing the cobblestones in the road three stories below us. This was so interesting that I ran to get my camera. Look, they are fixing cobblestones!

A few days later the mother admitted that she thought I would be a boring houseguest for being impressed by cobblestones.

I reached for the translation program. "In my town, we do not have cobblestones. Only boring paved roads."

I stood at the family's clothesline, handing wet clothes to the mother so she could hang them; I was afraid I'd drop the pieces three floors down to the neighbor's balcony. One day I asked the daughter what would happen if she dropped her underwear when she was hanging it on the clothesline.

She said that you say, "No mine." And buy more.

The Call to Prayer is broadcast five times a day from giant speakers in every town and city, at specific times. Each call unnerved me because it sounded like there was a man shouting into a megaphone. My first thought was always that there must be an emergency: a voice begging shoppers to run for their lives.

I'd been in the country for over a week, so knew that the voice was a reminder for people to stop whatever they were doing and pray, but was constantly startled when the quiet of a day was punctuated by a loud broadcast from speakers.

It could be heard everywhere in the city whether you were inside or far away from the center. Though this family is Muslim, they are more modern and do not stop to pray.

One day while the mother was hanging laundry, I stood next to her handing her articles of clothing. The Call to Prayer started, and my body tensed; the loud noise registered in my body as a distress signal and made me inhale fast and grab the mother's arm.

"Prayer," she said, laughing at me. "One prayer."

The call was so loud that we had to pause our conversation until it stopped several minutes later.

Once, the man's voice came through the speaker again, just a half hour after the regularly scheduled prayer. I knew something was wrong, very wrong.

I ran from the living room and found the mother in the kitchen drinking tea. I pointed in the air. "That voice," I said. "It is the wrong time."

She searched the ceiling where I pointed and shook her head at me. Then she heard the loud man's voice on the loudspeaker.

She laughed and spoke into the translation program. "He is reminding us to be kind."

I didn't ask her why he couldn't talk about kindness during his regular call.

I noted our similarities: clothes with English writing, a love of books and sports and good food, a love of travel, interesting work, the daughter fetching another glass of tea for her parents upon request, a love of higher education, children who spend as much time on the internet as children at home, and a love of farm-fresh food.

I noticed our differences: all food is truly farm fresh and vine ripened, they drink coffee and tea while sitting, they keep open jars of olives in the cupboard, eat plain yogurt at every meal, eat three vegetables to one protein, or no protein with their meals.

They buy bottled water for all drinking purposes and stop for tea every hour or so. The table is never set until you are ready to eat— even in restaurants. Stray cats and dogs are welcome everywhere, people care for stray animals by putting out food and water.

There are no top sheets on beds in hotels, which I sorely missed. Do you think hotels wash blankets after every guest?

I asked the family if they considered themselves more European or Asian, the question everyone always asks about Turkey since it lies on both continents. The archaeologist spoke into the translation program and said that they were more Mediterranean.

Of course they were, their diet was closer to a Mediterranean diet than anything else, but whenever I saw experts talking about the Mediterranean diet, they said that a portion of protein was a part of every meal.

I noticed that many meals here had little or no protein. Sure, you could buy it in restaurant meals, but the dinners I ate with friends often had no protein at all. It appeared that protein was for special occasions, like the day I arrived.

The family was patient as I asked question after question. I was equally patient when they asked many questions about my life.

"You celebrate the rabbit?" they asked.

I thought they were asking me if I ate rabbit meat, but then I caught their meaning. "Yes." I smiled. "My family celebrates Easter. We have an Easter egg hunt for the children to find hidden eggs and chocolate from the bunny."

The daughter thought they should visit for the Rabbit Day. I welcomed them to come any time, but the value of their currency is so low when compared to the dollar that there was no way they could ever save enough money to visit.

Years ago my friend Theresa noted that I punctuate the space around my sentences with the word, "Perfect." I didn't think much of it until I heard the mother, the archaeologist and the daughter each do that same thing within a few days of my arrival. Using the word "perfect" does not make a sentence perfect, but my verbal tick is now a part of their lexicon.

I insisted that my habits were not the final authority on United States culture and etiquette. "My country is so big, there is not one main food we all eat for breakfast." "My country has many different climates; where I live..." "Not everyone in my country celebrates Christmas, many people celebrate other holidays."

The daughter said to me during an English lesson, "Come to kitchen. Something big." I followed her into the kitchen, took one look at what was going on and said, "Oh my goodness."

The counter was filled with pots and pans and dishes and the table held an enormous amount of fruits, cooked and raw, and vegetables cooked and raw, and eggs and sausage and yogurt and cream and various jams. Their typical breakfasts have a lot of food, so seeing more than double that amount for a weekend feast amazed me.

While we ate, I added some rose jam to my yogurt for an intense combination of sweet and tart. The family watched me and murmured to each other in Turkish. The archaeologist watched me for a moment longer, then said, "Is good?" I smiled at the idea that making my own flavored yogurt was novel, and told them it was good.

After breakfast, the archaeologist asked me if I wanted to go to the bazaar; I thought he was suggesting that I buy a keychain of Turkey. I agreed to go but had no intention of buying trinkets.

The bazaar was a farmer's market; it was time to do the family's shopping for the next few days. Repeat: next few days. This was a farmer's market on steroids. Enormous piles of ripe food stacked on tables ready to be eaten; no need to set your peaches on a windowsill for a few days so they can ripen. This fact alone, that the foods are sold ripe, was a wonder.

He worked his way through the stalls, methodically choosing each piece of produce carefully, then stacking them in his wheeled cart and restacking the plastic bags with each purchase so the potatoes would not sit on the grapes.

Every stall offered a free taste and I gladly accepted a half of a peach here, a half of an apricot there, and a piece of cheese here and there.

I took out my journal as we walked around and took notes on what the father bought for us to eat: "18 large tomatoes. 4 kinds of cheese. 3 kinds of olives. 9 cucumbers. 4 eggplants. OMG: look at those ripe tomatoes!"

"That's a lot of tomatoes," I said to the mother when we got home. She counted them quickly. "No," she answered. "It right."

A building in the ancient city of Ephesus.

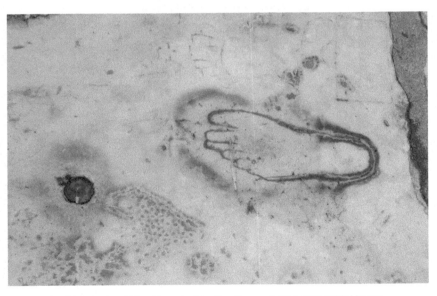

Looking for love? Continue in this direction and stop at the third house.

DAY 11 B: SELÇUK: EPHESUS

The archaeologist took me to Ephesus, a place I've wanted to go my whole adult life. The mother and daughter opted to stay home as they've been there many, many times. He managed Ephesus before he took the job of managing five museums in Izmir, so he knew everyone there.

They treated him like a celebrity and me like an expected guest. We were waved through lines, invited behind the scenes, and one of his friends moved our car to the staff parking lot while we explored so we wouldn't have to walk the long road back to retrieve it at the end.

I couldn't believe I got to tour Ephesus with one of its top experts.

The ancient city itself was sprawling and surrounded by plush trees and flowers and mountains. It was humbling to stand around pieces of history: columns, walls, sidewalks, roads and parts of statues that are waiting for the missing pieces to be returned to them.

There is an ongoing effort to retrieve the missing parts that were robbed from the site and sold to museums around the world. The archaeologist requested that if in my world travels, I ever saw something from Ephesus in a museum in another country, to please let him know.

I promised him that I would, but worried that unless the statue had a sign that read, "Stolen from Ephesus" I'd likely have no idea of its origins.

As we walked into the site, I noticed that the relics here were just like the pieces I'd seen in the museum yesterday. I wanted to say, "That piece should be in the museum, too."

Ephesus was a major Greek city from the tenth century BC but became known when the Romans took over in 129 BC.

Large buildings in crumbles. Bits of mosaics on the floors. Stairs leading to the upstairs of a municipal building that we climbed. Pieces of wallpaper and shadows of frescos. Knowing that the place had been ransacked and broken apart by people for centuries, I was amazed that there was so much left.

A main rocky road ran through the city with pieces of buildings and statues lined up along its edges. I listened to English-speaking guides around us explaining the city to their tour groups, but their information was either incorrect or lacking important details.

I pointed to one guide who led a group of older Americans and said to my archaeologist via the translation program, "He is making things up."

"Like?"

"He told them that Jesus lived here."

The archaeologist shook his head. "No." He watched the guide for a few moments, then said, "I think people no remember words."

Mary, Jesus's mother, spent the final years of her life nearby. We visited the site earlier. Perhaps that's what the guide should have said?

I turned my focus to my friend's teachings.

He used every English word he could think of to explain this wonder of the ancient world to me. He matched words together and tried to use the translation program to explain things, but the internet wasn't very strong there.

I wished I spoke Turkish so I could understand everything.

He showed me the ancient outdoor public bathroom with long rows of holes right next to each other for men and women to relieve themselves, without separation or privacy. He used the translation program, "This bathroom was only for distinguished people, not for slaves or farmers."

The front wall of the Library of Celsus, the most impressive site, was still standing tall. I wondered how many scrolls were kept there in its prime.

I asked him how many scrolls.

He opened his arms all the way to show a large number and said, "Big."

I wrote the number 15,000 in my journal, and was unsure later if he said that's how many scrolls were kept there or perhaps he was saying that was the most that could be kept there. I decided it didn't matter.

There was an ongoing restoration called the Terrace House that once connected six houses of the uber-wealthy. There were bits of frescos on the walls, parts of mosaics on the floors and chunks of arched walls that remained intact.

The houses were now protected by enormous sheets of plastic, so we the public could not destroy or deface them.

Several tables held hundreds of pieces of marble. My archaeologist explained that endlessly patient and optimistic archaeologists (who were not present when I visited) worked to puzzle the many pieces of marble back into a wall. I wondered how many years they had worked to rebuild this crumbled wall.

From dust to wall? The implausibility of that venture made me think of the children's chant, "All the king's horses and all the king's men couldn't put Humpty Dumpty back together again."

How many years had they been working to restore that wall?

Ten years.

This area that's roped off from the public demonstrates what being an archaeologist is like: painstakingly intricate work. I'd prefer to reach my hand into the sand and pull out the proverbial golden teapot.

While climbing around upstairs in the Terrace House, my archaeologist looked around and saw we were alone. He pointed to a hallway, "You go. Fast. Careful."

I stepped over a rope and tiptoed down the hall, and walked into an empty room that had all four walls and the ceiling intact, which was amazing when you think about how many thousands of years old this room was.

Then I saw the art. The fresco on the ceiling was the most

preserved piece of art I'd seen on the trip, seconded only by the mosaic on the floor. I looked back at my friend and put my hands on my face and opened my mouth for an exaggerated state of awe, because I wanted him to know that I understood the magnificence of this room.

He nodded fast, and then waved me back.

He took me to the staff room, a small and dark room with an old refrigerator on one side. He opened the fridge and got us each a small bottle of water, which was great because I'd already drunk the water I brought with me. This cold water was a treat on such a hot and dusty day.

We went back outside where he pointed out things I would have missed.

"This foot and heart," he said as we stood over an unnoticed area on the side of a road. "See toe three big?"

"Yes."

"This if you look love. Come house three from this."

Oh. So in pointing to the small painting of a foot and a heart on the side of the road, the third toe was longer, which meant if you went to the third house down, you would find a prostitute.

I laughed.

"You understand?"

"I understand."

In the building after the library, the archaeologist pointed to some writing on the wall that described the sarcophagus of a notable man. I read about his life in English on the sign.

Then he got down on his hands and knees in front of a small, unmarked grate in the wall. "He here," he pointed, insisting I take his place next to the grate. I got on my knees and bent down with my cheek on the floor to look through the grate. Musty smell. Dark. I waited a moment to see if my eyes would adjust, and they did: I could make out a round piece that looked like an emblem.

"You see?" he asked.

I answered, "I see something round."

He nodded. "Yes. That he."

It's one thing to read a sign that explains that this building was built to honor an important man; it's another to lay my cheek on the dirty floor and see the man's tomb.

He told me every story about every building, using his beautifully broken English until my eyes glazed over. I didn't think I could hear one more story about one more old thing.

"We go now," he said; we left and drove home.

I took a shower before dinner so I wouldn't dirty their apartment from the dust that clung to my body and clothes and hair.

I've traveled with a small carry-on suitcase for this trip. I had three short-sleeved shirts that I wore on rotation, but on this leg of the trip I wore two of the shirts on repeat. I'd wear one, then wash it and let it dry while I wore the other.

Tonight I wore the third shirt and the family gasped when I joined them for dinner.

I was glad to add a little "wow" into their lives, too.

Photo next page: Holly Winter Huppert explores Ephesus.

The mother of the family walks along the upper castle wall. (Note: no railing)

A stone room in the Basilica of St. John where St. John spent his final years writing his part of the Bible.

DAY 12: SELÇUK: CASTLE

"You ready now?" the mother asked first thing in the morning. I leapt to attention, thinking I had another half hour until we were leaving. I was never sure what I needed for our days together, so threw a hat, a scarf, sunscreen and my purse into my day bag and ran out the door after the family.

We met the English teacher, her husband and their long-haired daughter at a park for breakfast. The English teacher brought a tablecloth that fit the picnic table perfectly.

"Did you buy this cloth for this table?" I asked.

She laughed. "No. It's a lucky fit."

It's lucky to have a friend who is Turkish and speaks perfect English. I save most of my culture questions for her.

The only word that stumped her in our many, many conversations was "Bickee."

We'd been talking about going to a *hamam*, a Turkish bath. She said some people wear a bick-ee.

"I don't know what that is."

She said it again, "Bick-ee."

I shrugged and asked her if it were a kind of bathrobe.

She took out her phone and typed it in English. "Bikini."

"Oh," I said. "Bikini, that's a bathing suit."

She repeated it several times to perfect her pronunciation, then continued the conversation.

Our breakfast feast had included my favorites: eggs, yogurt, cream, red paste, cheeses, assorted olives, bread, several kinds of jam and sliced tomatoes, cucumbers and green peppers.

"Why is there jam with breakfast?" I asked the English teacher.

"You mix the jam with the cheese, it's the healthiest kind of cheese because it's boiled. And some people eat the jam with bread."

Note to self: Stop using cucumber slices to scoop up jam. Eat the jam with cheese.

After breakfast I went for a walk with the mother and the archaeologist. We meandered around the lake. A stray dog swam in the lake and then decided, as all dogs do, that the best place to shake off the water would be right next to us.

Thanks, dog.

We moved the picnic place to the shade and the archaeologist set up a hammock for the daughter and her long-haired friend. Once we were all settled and the other adults had fresh cups of tea, the girls read aloud from their new favorite book, *Green Eggs and Ham*. Those tongue twisters weren't confusing them anymore; amazing what a little practice can do.

After a while, the archaeologist kicked the girls out of the hammock so he might have a nap, and I teased the mother and the English teacher that it was their turn to read in English. They decided that we should dance, instead.

"First the 'Penguin Dance,'" the English teacher said. We lined up congo-style and the English teacher's husband started the music. Leg touch to the right. Leg touch to the left. Hop forward. Hop backwards. Three hops forward.

Well, well. We were doing the "Bunny Hop."

We laughed and hopped around our spot of shade. When we were done, I insisted on finding the American version of the song and we danced the same moves to a different tune.

And so started the Turkish cultural dance lessons. The English teacher's husband found a song, and we women and young girls stood in a circle. The music played. Step one way three times, then back and forth three times, then three touches with your foot and five claps—low to high. Repeat. Repeat. We laughed and danced, and tried to keep up with the music as it got faster.

They played and performed dances from the different regions of Turkey after I watched examples on YouTube. In one region the women seemed to float next to the men. In another region the men wore what looked like military uniforms, and sometimes women performed in those uniforms, but you couldn't tell it was women until the very end when they took off their hats.

I watched a dance troupe from the northern parts of Turkey. Their dance moves reminded me of a Russian dance.

"That's because that part of Turkey is closer to Russia," the English teacher's husband said. "You understand that borders don't define people, right?"

I nodded.

He said, "People mix different cultures with those who live near them."

We spent the afternoon at home relaxing; the fast-paced touring schedule had exhausted us all. After dinner the father said, "We go the Basilica of St. John."

I nodded in agreement.

"Now," he said. "We go now."

I helped clean the table, grabbed my bag and off we went. The daughter was still tired and decided to stay home where she could play games on the internet with her friends.

We started the ten-minute walk to the basilica. The mother kept humming a tune. I hummed with her. The father played the song on his phone: it was the Edith Piaf song, "Padam Padam." We three sang along as we walked; when the song ended, we walked quietly, then one of us would start humming and we'd all be singing the chorus again. The mother and I waltzed together while we waited for the light. Padam Padam.

The staff of the basilica greeted the father warmly and we entered through a side gate. I was immediately enthralled with the columns and pieces of wall lying on the ground. We walked up the walkway and the father said the excavation house was closed, but we would go in anyway.

"Now you meet the people."

Inside we were greeted by a friend of the father and some interns from college; they lived on-site. They fed us ice cream and fruit and were not insulted that I didn't want tea. I thought the men were talking about museum stuff in Turkish, like how many people walked through the site today, or the punishment for a tourist who posed from behind a statue, or how many new sculptures had been unearthed in the garden today.

But then I heard the father say in a high voice, "Oh my goodness!" and it became clear that I was the topic of these highly educated people. I laughed along with them and wondered how often I said that phrase, one of the side-effects of teaching kindergarten.

Time to overhaul my speaking patterns.

We left the friends and made our way through the church of St. John, as the father told me story after story and photographed the mother and me against every possible backdrop.

"You are a good archaeologist," I said to him.

"Yes," he answered.

"One day you will stop that and be a photographer," I said.

He laughed for a long time.

"Yes," his wife said. "Good archaeologist. Good photographer. Good husband. Good father. Good man."

I nodded in agreement.

"You want see castle?" the father asked.

Yes.

The guard gave him the keys to the castle, which was already closed.

The mother looked at me. "Keys to castle."

"Now my house," I said, and we laughed.

Gigantic wooden doors with one keyhole. We entered and stood in the center of the inside of the castle. Most of the innards were gone, few inner walls, no roof, but there were many piles of rocks. The outer wall surrounding the castle stood tall, which seemed odd since this was the part of the castle that invaders attacked first. We walked around and climbed on things and stayed in awe of the history around us.

I'm not sure who started it: Padam Padam. The mother and I danced where the floor of the castle once was, perhaps an old ballroom. We laughed, then got back to exploring.

The father said, "We go. Very careful. Up."

He started climbing the crumbling stone steps to the very top of the outer wall, where you might shoot arrows down on invaders. The steps were narrow and steep, and pieces of rock came loose and fell to their death as he climbed up. There was nothing to keep you from slipping over the edge on the left side of the staircase.

I hesitated. The mother took my day bag and slung it over her shoulder. Up I went, hugging the inside wall and studying the steps so I might see a loose stone before I stepped wrong. I got to the top and tried to ignore my racing heart; this was the highest I had ever climbed without a safety net of some kind, or a railing or a wall.

I stood along the narrow ridge admiring the view. Again there was no railing and nothing to keep me from tumbling over the edge. Good thing I wasn't afraid of heights.

Falling. That was my fear when standing four stories up on a narrow ledge that's not part of the general tour. Mind you, I wasn't afraid of dying from a fall, only afraid of the fall itself.

"Be very. Up careful." The father motioned to me as he walked along the ridge where only one side had a small wall to help keep your feet positioned on the ridge.

We're walking on top of the wall.

My legs quivered as I followed behind him. He turned to snap my photograph; I smiled the kind of smile you make when you are terrified.

The mother smiled and posed. She wasn't as nervous about being up there; likely she'd been up there before.

We stopped and admired the view from wider vantage points. Music wafted up to us from the valley below, and the mother belly-danced to the music on that narrow ledge, which was amazing since she was still carrying my day bag.

When we made it to the far side of the castle, the father asked if we wanted to go down the easy way or the hard way. The fact that he asked scared me. I looked at the mother and she said some harsh words to him in Turkish. He turned and jumped off our wall and onto another wall.

I looked at the mother. We stood rooted in our place. He called back to us in Turkish and pointed to places we could climb down. The first ledge was the most difficult to scramble down. Once we got our footing, we had a few more ledges to drop onto as we made our way down; I missed that crumbling staircase from earlier. Slowly we made our way back to solid ground.

"This is it," the father said as we walked around to the side. "Read information, in English." We laughed and I read the sign.

St. John spent his last days in this room when he was 90 years old, praying and writing his part of the Bible.

It's one thing to know the Bible is filled with stories, but it's another thing to walk into those stories and see the vistas that historic figure saw and touch the place where he sat to pray and write.

"You pray here," the father said as he and the mother walked out.

I didn't explain to him that I didn't go to church and didn't really know St. John's stories, but in their view, I was not Muslim, so then I must be a practicing Christian. This room was a pilgrimage site for Christians from around the world.

I sat and looked around. A well. Rocks leaning every way. But you could still make out that this was a room of sorts.

I meditated for a few minutes, then gushed my gratitude for being in Turkey and for finding people on my journey who felt like family. I gave thanks for my continued safety on my trip and asked for a blessing on the children of the world, especially the hungry ones and the ones who were fleeing war zones and seeking asylum in my country, as was reported in the news at this time.

On the way out we with sat with the excavation team again, and watched as the sun prepared to set.

One of the interns had practiced English while we were away and asked, "Do you drink mint and lemon tea?"

I was honored that they worked so hard to please me, and readily accepted the warm drink made especially for me.

From my vantage point I could hear them speaking Turkish around me, I could see the one remaining column of Artemis's temple, the mosque next to it and the valley below St. John's as the sun slowly fell.

The mother asked me if I was bored.

No, not at all. I could sit here all day and absorb the beauty around me.

We shook hands with each intern before we left, and on the way out the mother said, "My friend library. We go?"

"Okay." I had no idea what she suggested, but it didn't matter. I was up for anything.

"We go now?" she asked.

"Yes," I said. Every time I think the day is over, there's always one more chapter.

The father's phone rang, and I recognized the song. "Padam Padam."

The mother smiled as I recognized the tune.

The father showed me a video of the two of them dancing to that song in Paris. They had been together/married for nineteen years and their favorite song was alive and well in their lives.

"Your song," I said.

"Yes," the mother smiled.

We removed our shoes before entering the home of the librarian and her guests, as is customary in Turkey. We sat and ate roasted chickpeas and peanuts and the conversation flowed in English and Turkish.

The librarian asked me, "Why did you come to Turkey?"

I wanted to say that I came to have a picnic with friends in the park. I came to relax away an afternoon. I came to climb the upper ridge of a castle. I came to watch the sun set over sacred ground. I came to eat roasted chickpeas with new friends.

But I ended up saying something about adventure.

Adventure was part of the reason, too.

Holly Winter Huppert teaching the song, "Miss Mary Mack" to the daughter of the family she stayed with.

The daughter of the family is playing the piano while her friend with the long hair sings along.

DAY 13: SELÇUK: TEACHING

At breakfast I got into a conversation with the family about the difference between seeds and pits. In Turkish there is one word to represent both things.

I got a piece of paper and listed the seeds on our breakfast table: watermelon, cucumber, pepper, and the pits: olives, peach, date.

They didn't know the word date in English, so I found a photo which led to a discussion on the different uses for the word date: 1. the fruit, 2. a day on the calendar, 3. a romantic outing.

The mother asked what "pet" meant; I wrote out a flight of words, pat, pet, pit, pot, put. I drew pictures next to each word and then we each demonstrated the difference between petting and patting on the daughter's head.

"Why are you touch me now when the word is pot?" the daughter asked her father.

He corrected himself and petted, then patted, her head again.

We moved the English lesson to the floor where we sat in a circle on the carpet. The daughter and I taught the mother and the father how to sing and do the hand movements to the children's song, "Miss Mary Mack" that the daughter and I have been working on. I know that this song doesn't have a practical application to carry them forward in their mastery of English. When will they ever need to use the phrase, "With silver buttons, buttons, buttons all down her back, back, back"?

The daughter chose to be at the piano for her English lesson, where she practiced the song, "If the Stars Were Mine." She could play the piano part beautifully and was memorizing the words and getting that off-beat start to the song. She hadn't complained once that she wasn't learning a Katy Perry song.

I couldn't resist teaching her the instrumental piano song, "Heart and Soul." It's the only song my mother banned from our house for the boring melody line that plays over and over like a skip on a record. The daughter loved the song and learned the left-hand part quickly; we had some more work to do on the right hand.

With so many children in my house growing up, we could get a sibling to take over playing without stopping the song and would keep it going for hours, which would drive my mother nearly to insanity.

The daughter mastered the basics, and if she teaches the song to one friend, it's possible that this song, too, can annoy the mothers of Turkey.

"You want to try it again?" I asked.

"Yes," she whispered, and started from the beginning.

It's almost time for me to leave my friends, and this makes me sad. I've found people who feel like family and a big part of me wants to stay. I wanted to go over some writing in the father's museums, but I could do that from the road. I would have enjoyed helping the mother set up her classroom for the fall, but the municipality was still renovating her building. If I had one more week, I could have helped the daughter get the "v" sound out of her "w" words, as in "Vye you vant vater so much?"

Later when we were out, the mother, the father and I had a discussion on whether a stray kitten was cute, as in "cute cat" or lovely, as in "lovely cat." I suggested that the cat was cute, but the mother was lovely.

The father repeated that phrase quietly, "Lovely mother. Lovely mother." He was quiet for a few minutes then said again, "Lovely mother."

The word he had trouble remembering was "mosquito." Every time the father was bitten by one, he asked how to say that bad word again.

"Mosquito," I'd say slowly, then add, "Those insects are helping you learn English."

The father repeated, "mosquito" then looked up a word in the translate program. "Abundance of mosquitoes." That phrase was so cute that I didn't correct him or suggest a change. Rather I walked around with a faraway look on my face while saying, "An abundance of mosquitoes," and nodding as if in agreement.

In the afternoon we headed to a pool in the mountains where the air was cooler. There were no other buildings around; we were surrounded by wilderness. The daughter invited a few friends, a brother and a sister, and they splashed around while her mother and the archaeologist read a book translated from English on raising a gifted child.

I sat in the shade and did nothing for hours. I didn't ask any questions or document anything. My camera never left my bag. I didn't read or write. I watched the children playing the way all children play at the pool.

They splashed each other. They dunked each other. They swam to collect things from the bottom. They jumped off the edge into the deep end repeatedly. They stopped for computer breaks to make videos of themselves laughing and drinking water, then left the computer to jump back into the water, shrieking at the cold temperature.

The brother threw the goggles over the edge that was a five-foot drop to the ground below. He asked me what he should do.

I pointed to the office and typed into the translate program, "Tell them in the office."

The children love the computer voice of the translation program, and love to repeat the words so they sound as robotic as the computer.

"Tell them in the office," the brother repeated, flatly.

We left the pool and drove deeper into the mountains and arrived at a center with a restaurant and campgrounds. We found a spot, unloaded the food and set up the table with the picnic foods we brought with us. The center gave us a tablecloth, then the owner returned with a small black grill filled with smoking hot charcoal and placed it next to our table.

What an interesting business idea: rent hot charcoal grills to picnickers.

A few wasps found us, yellow jackets. We ignored them and set the table. Within minutes more wasps found us and crawled all over the meat. Seriously? I thought this might be the most wasps I had ever seen at one time, but they were just starting. More arrived. Then more. And more still.

The children were swarmed by wasps, so they left us to play with a zipline that was just off the ground. The mother and I covered the meat with hand towels that she brought along, but the wasps found their way to the meat. The father grilled the meat and we shooed wasps away to no avail.

It was a wasp apocalypse.

We made plates for the children and carried the food to the center's covered deck area next to the lake. We enjoyed ten minutes of quiet before the wasps found us. I helped cover the plates with flat bread, but the wasps wouldn't leave. The children left the area and I did my best to throw their uneaten food into the garbage so we might get some peace.

I returned to the grill. The father had several stings on his hand and his neck that were swelling. The mother and I looked from his neck to each other. We packed the car and shooed the wasps out of the trunk, then walked Father to the center's office and sat him down. The mother held ice on his neck, and we noticed the back of his hand was swelling, too.

We left and as the father drove us home, the children complained that they were hungry, but they didn't want to eat anything when we got home. They wanted to go out for ice cream.

Not tonight.

The father relaxed with ice cubes on his hand and the mother and I sat on the balcony with cups of herbal tea.

We used one phone and translated thoughts back and forth at a rapid pace, only stalling when the program accidentally changed languages or misrepresented what we wanted to say.

We went deeper into our stories. She talked about her low blood pressure and how she had too many interests and didn't like to rest, which the doctor wanted her to do. I told her that I had low blood pressure, too, but that my doctor told me to stay active and eat more salt. We decided that perhaps the answer was somewhere in the middle for both of us.

The father came out to refresh our tea and showed us that his swelling had gone down, then he returned to his bedroom to read.

I told the mother that I was sad to leave her family.

She agreed and told me that we are now a family. She thought for a moment, then typed into the phone, "But I know you and have watched you. You are the happiest when you can see something new and write about it."

I nodded in agreement.

We picked up our phones and she plotted my journey around Turkey for the next month. She came up with a plan where I would have mostly 3-hour bus rides, then stop for two nights in a new area. According to our schedule, I had one more full day with the family.

When we were too exhausted to continue, I used simple words that she could understand without help from the translation program: "A good day."

She corrected my English. "Many good days."

DAY 14: SELÇUK: JOKE

Today the daughter and her long-haired friend and I walked across town. The friend said she had a joke to tell me. I was always up for a joke, especially when it encouraged the girls to use their English.

"So." The long-haired friend smiled and stopped walking so she could concentrate on her words. "There were two tomatoes that wanted to cross the road."

I figured this was going to be some version of "Why did the chicken cross the road?" or something to do with ketchup, so I willed myself to be surprised at a simple answer.

The friend continued, "And the first tomato said that he could cross the road, no problem. So he waited until there was a break in the traffic and started crossing the road. A car hit him, and he died."

I put my hands over my heart. "When you said this was a joke, I didn't know it was a sad joke. Please tell me that the first tomato came back to life."

Both girls shook their heads to show the poor tomato was gone forever.

I said, "Did the second tomato have a funeral for the first tomato?"

"No," the friend said, quickly.

I said, "No funeral? Poor first tomato. I hope this story is going to end on a happy note."

The friend ignored me and continued, "So the second tomato said he could cross the street. He stepped out into traffic, got hit by a car and died."

My mouth fell open. "This is the saddest joke I ever heard. Seriously? Both tomatoes died?"

The daughter and her friend smiled big smiles. "Yes," the friend said. "They both died."

I said, "Is this a popular joke in Turkey?"

"Yes," both girls smiled.

We stood on the sidewalk looking at each other. This felt like one of those jokes natives play on visitors to their country.

I said, "So. This is the whole joke? Two dead tomatoes?"

The friend said, "Well, there is one more word."

I waited.

"When the second friend died, he said 'Aroot.'" (Written phonetically.)

"Why did he say that?" I asked.

"He just said it."

"What does it mean?" I asked.

The girls looked at each other. "I don't know the word in English," they chorused.

"Is it an important word in the story?" I asked.

"Yes," the friend said.

"Can I understand the story without the word?"

"No," the friend said.

Okay. So that happens sometimes when children tell a joke. They get the joke wrong or get the punchline wrong, but losing the meaning of the last and essential word? That's a new one.

I laughed with them, yeah...good one.

In order to prove there were no hard feelings for being told a joke with such a terrifying ending and no punch line, I decided to tell them the chicken crossing the road joke.

"Do you want to hear a joke?" I asked.

The girls nodded a yes.

"Why did the chicken cross the road?

The girls said together, "I don't know."

I spoke slowly and clearly so they could get the punch line. "To get to the other side."

With that the two girls turned from me and walked towards our destination.

I smiled from behind them, "Do you understand?"

I had to walk quickly to keep up with them.

The daughter said, "That joke is not good."

"Not good?" I said. "At least the chicken lived."

The girls were so annoyed by my joke they refused to look at me as we walked to the café.

We met the long-haired friend's mother, the English teacher, at a café and ordered a delicious gluten-free lunch for all of us to share. A jar of homemade yogurt came with the meal, and I copied my friends and dripped yogurt over the other foods, piled some in a lump and ate it with a "soup" spoon.

I asked the English teacher about the tomato joke and she laughed so hard at the girls not knowing the last word that she couldn't speak for a few moments. Finally she calmed herself enough to relate, "That is a joke to teach children to be careful when you cross the street, so you don't end up like the tomatoes."

I nodded. So it wasn't a joke, it was a cautionary tale.

Got it.

The owner of the café gave us another jar of yogurt and I spilled more onto my plate. "I love eating yogurt with everything."

The English teacher explained that yogurt takes away the fried oil taste in the food.

I nodded slowly at this new information.

"I've never been good at making yogurt," I said as I ate another dollop of the café's homemade delicacy. "Whenever I try, I end up with a giant pot of milk. And I don't like milk."

The English teacher said the best yogurt is made with sheep's milk.

I thought that was an exciting tip and might have dubbed it the "Tip of the Day," but then I ordered a glass of lemonade. It came in a tall glass with a few pieces of ice. It wasn't sweet, it wasn't sour. It's as if the very definition of what lemonade is supposed to be bloomed inside of me. So, this is lemonade.

We were in a small locally owned café that opened a week ago. The English teacher explained how they made the lemonade.

Lemonade from the Queen Bee Cafe:
  Grate the lemon rind.
  Squeeze all the juice of the lemons into the lemon rind.
  Add just enough sugar ***
  Let the concoction sit on the counter for a day
  Add water to a glass. Add some of the lemon juice concoction.

I know, that part of the recipe that called for some questionable amount of sugar depending on the size and bitterness of the lemons just didn't work for me. I planned to revisit this cafe every few hours until my bus left tomorrow, so I might better understand this lemonade process.

We left the café and walked around the city. We went into the Isa Bey Mosque and were again surrounded by the history of this city. I was asked to cover my head with scarves they had clipped to clothes hangers and to put on a purple bathrobe just to walk around the lobby.

The English teacher and the girls weren't made to wear robes, but borrowed head coverings, just for fun, as we stood in the lobby and considered the beauty of the mosque.

We walked around the city and looked into shop windows and down long alleys while I listened to the stories of the city the English teacher told me. After a while we returned to the same café, which I thought was a really good idea because, you know, lemonade. I showed great restraint by only ordering one more; I drank it as fast as I could and wasn't sorry.

The mother and the archaeologist joined us. The archaeologist asked what I thought about the mosque, then told me that they believed parts of the building were built with parts of the Artemis Temple and pieces from the Basilica of St. John. There was also a thought that Apollo's tomb was buried under the mosque's floor, which made me want to go back there after dark...to have a better look around.

He slapped his arm as we talked. "Mosquito."

My eyes opened wider. "You learned how to say mosquito!"

"Mosquitoes and wasps like me," he said.

The mother said, "Sweet husband."

We laughed.

The mothers and daughters and I decided to continue the late-night party, because in Selçuk there's always another chapter, and went to a café on the other side of town.

Sitting at a table were the librarian and her friends from our visit a few nights before. We joined them and ordered more drinks, water for me, tea for everyone else.

The librarian and her sister showed me pictures of beautiful gardens that were near their father's house, where they are going for a holiday. They invited me to come and stay with them later in the week. I accepted their offer, glad I hadn't booked my hotel room yet.

I hoped they didn't want help with the gardening because I'm not much of a gardener.

The librarian and her sister invited the mother and me to attend an international breakfast in the morning. We accepted.

Next to the café, the English teacher showed me a statue of Mustafa Kemal Atatürk, the founder and first president of Turkey. She shared the history of him taking over Turkey in 1923 and how his policies—workers' rights, women's rights and children's rights—brought Turkey into the modern age.

She shared one of his favorite quotes. I thought it worked well over one hundred years later and summed up what I wanted most, as I spent my last night sitting with new friends and choosing yet another café to stop at before we closed my last night in Selçuk.

"Yurtta Sulh, cihanda sulh" Atatürk (1931)

"Peace at home. Peace in the world."

The mother waves goodbye to the author as she heads to Denizli on the train.

Words in English stating that the next station is Denizli.

DAY 15: DENIZLI: TRAIN

I used the GPS on my phone to help me find the international breakfast the librarian was hosting at her library. I enjoyed walking along the streets of Selçuk by myself.

I arrived at the breakfast to a table covered with many small dishes of food. Will I ever get used to the colorful Turkish breakfasts? The librarian knew all ten of us guests, but we didn't know each other. The mother of the family I was staying with did not come; she wasn't feeling well.

Luckily the language of the breakfast was English. There were several people from the librarian's church who were from the United States. I enjoyed hearing their perspectives on the country.

We ate and compared travel stories and were treated to some musical performances. A man played the *ney*, a traditional Turkish flute. The simple melody pulled the group together and I felt like I was in not just my happy place, but in a happy trance.

"Yes," someone in the group said when I mentioned the mystical feeling to the music. "This is the instrument they play for the whirling dervishes." I would be visiting the whirling dervishes in a few weeks and would look forward to hearing that music again.

The librarian gave me a tour of the library she runs on the site.

People from all over Turkey have sent books for her to loan to anyone in the mood to read.

She said, "I think books should be available to anyone."

Most of the books were in Turkish; it was funny to see *Bridget Jones's Diary* with a Turkish cover sporting a dark-haired woman.

"I liked this book," I said to her sister. "I like to read diaries."

"Yes," she smiled. "And now we are reading your travel diary of Turkey."

I returned to the house where I have stayed for the past week and was relieved to see the mother eating a simple breakfast. She had to go to the hospital last night and was still weak, but she looked a lot better than she did when she got home this morning.

I told her about the breakfast and how the librarian had to walk me almost all the way home, because I was so accustomed to hanging out with the family that I didn't know her address.

The mother laughed.

I got her a glass of water which she reluctantly accepted with a thank-you. "You must drink," I said into the translate program and refilled the glass when she was finished. "Dehydration is a serious problem."

She pointed to the water. "No like water."

I mimed an IV in her arm. "Water good. IV not good."

She nodded and sipped the water with a frown.

I was packing when the daughter came into my room.

She said, "Do you want to go with my mother to a café?"

"Yes," I said, surprised that the mother was going out.

"We go now," the daughter said.

The mother drove and we dropped the daughter off with her friends, and one of Mother's friends, a literature teacher, joined us. The mother stopped to pick up her prescription and then we drove to the same café where we hung out yesterday.

I ate a rice pudding, creamy, sweet, fresh milk, with cinnamon. In leaving my new friends, I'm going to be on my own again in figuring out what is gluten-free. It was good to learn that I could eat the rice pudding in Turkey. I ordered a lemonade and that freshly steeped drink was like an exclamation point on my stay in Sleek: just right.

We drove by the bus station and the literature teacher helped me talk to the ticket agent so I could buy a ticket for the 4:30 bus. The same man who told me yesterday that I didn't need a reservation or to buy my ticket ahead of time said today that I needed a reservation and should have bought my ticket already; the bus was full.

Really?

"Is full," the literature teacher said.

I sighed and asked if there was a train. Yes, 16:53. But the trains were notoriously full; likely I would have to stand for three hours.

I sighed.

"Don't worry," I said into the translate program when we got home. "I am from New York. If there is a seat on that train, it is mine."

The mother went with me to the train station. I slipped the ticket to Denizli into my back pocket and we sat on a ledge waiting.

I couldn't explain the level of comfort and attachment and love I felt for this family I'd only met a week ago. The mother told people I was a sister; I felt that too.

"It is so comfortable with you," the mother said into the translate program.

"Like a family," I said.

We sat quietly for a few minutes.

I spoke into the translate program, "Promise me you will take care of yourself. Drink water."

She nodded. She spoke into the program. "You be careful. And call me if you need anything. I can help from far away."

I nodded.

We could hear the train coming. Transitions in train stations are swift. I gave her a hug and said thank you three times while looking into her eyes; she nodded slowly. I lined up behind a woman so nobody could get in front of me. When the door opened the woman waited for the many people to get off. I lifted my even heavier suitcase, thanks to the new book of poetry the librarian gifted me with, and climbed aboard.

It's always a quandary when entering a busy train: which way do I turn? Where are the empty seats? The woman in front of me turned right, so I turned left. I walked halfway through the packed car and found an aisle seat.

Score!

The mother stood outside the window and I motioned that I got a seat. I waved goodbye to my friend and then lifted my suitcase over my head onto the rack above the seats.

And that's how chapters end, and new ones begin.

The train pulled out of the station and I got that familiar feeling of wondering if I was on the right train. You know, what if? Since the mother helped me find my way it was highly likely, but the thing with train travel is that there isn't anyone to ask what train this is. And besides, nobody spoke English.

Note to self: Next time carry a timetable.

I settled in for the three-hour ride. Every time I was close to sleeping, I would think about how amazing it was that I was in Turkey and would wake up again. Turkey. I was in Turkey. Could you believe that I was traveling through Turkey!

I punched the name of the city I was going to into my GPS and found that I still had hours to travel.

I studied the landscapes from the window.

Sweeping countryside vistas of the valley with mountains standing guard over us all. We stopped in small stations for people to get on or off and the train itself became a metaphor for life, choosing to move or choosing to sit and watch the world move, or moving at triple speed to get to the next thing faster.

The man who sat next to me moved to a different seat and a young woman wearing long sleeves, long slacks and a head scarf sat next to me.

She seemed to be about the age of the daughter of the family I'd just left in Selçuk. I turned to smile at the girl, and she looked away.

Okay. No problem.

The girl picked up her phone and started taking selfies of herself and out of the corner of my eye, I saw that she was posting them on Instagram. At one point she sneezed, and I automatically said, "Bless you." She looked at me and smiled, then picked up her phone and tapped away.

After another hour or so the girl continued taking selfies but made sure I was always in the background. I kept a half-smile on my face so I wouldn't appear to be scowling. Soon she was taking videos. Of me. At profile, which is not my best angle. I wondered if she would talk to me and try to get an interview for her page. I sat and relaxed and let her film more video footage of me than has been collectively recorded in my life.

Is this Karma for the many photos I've taken of others over the past few weeks?

I booked my hotel room through a site called, "Turkey Travel Planner." For the city I was visiting, they recommended two hotels. A good one and a two-star one. Both were next to the bus station, which was convenient. The better one had no vacancies. The two-star one boasted "unfussy" rooms for a mere $15 a night.

Unfussy rooms?

I didn't expect much, but they were ready for me when I arrived. One of the young men at the desk rolled my suitcase and led me into the elevator. He hit the third-floor button when we got inside, and all the lights in the elevator went off.

Not the warm welcome I was hoping for.

The lights went back on in an instant. The man looked at me and laughed, as I may have looked a little tense.

"No problem," he laughed some more. "No problems, no."

Though the room was far better than expected with a bathroom, working lights, a comfortable bed with a working phone next to it, air conditioning, a refrigerator (!) and a balcony (!), the thing that resonated with me the most was the declaration from the young man in the elevator.

"No problems. No."

A view in Pamukkale

St. Philip's Fountain at the ancient city of Hierapolis.

DAY 16: DENIZLI: PAMUKKALE

I retraced my footsteps. I must have missed it. This was a bus station, there had to be a ticket office. I'd walked the top floor along both sides of the building, searching. I walked the bottom floor. No ticket office.

Where was it? I tried to follow the kinds of people who might be looking to buy a bus ticket—the lady with two young children? No, they were riding the escalator down to catch a bus. The businessman walking swiftly? No, he was heading to security.

I looked for the word ticket (*bilet*) or ticketing (*biletlendirme*) or ticket office (*bilet gisesi*) but there wasn't anything, upstairs or downstairs. There was nobody to ask; I could use my translate program with a vendor if I really, really had to.

"Where can I buy a bus ticket?"

The center of the bus station was an open courtyard where people walked around or sat for a rest. Along the side walls there were two rows of buses with permanent gate numbers hung above the parking place, as if the bus won a prize at the country fair: "56" or "117."

I found a map posted on a wall upstairs that showed where each gate number was located, in case you were searching for your bus, but no mention of the ticket office. It's a good thing I found that posting, because I'd need it one day if I had a ticket and wanted to leave on a bus.

I wanted to buy a ticket for Saturday's bus to Isparta where I would meet the sisters, so I wouldn't risk the bus filling before I had a seat. I walked the entire upstairs and then the downstairs, again, trying to look like I needed help.

Not this time; I was on my own.

There weren't any throngs of people walking towards one place, as you might expect in an enormous two-floor bus station with an escalator in the center and elevators along the edges.

If I were a ticket office...

I went back upstairs and decided to walk behind the rows of buses, the only place I hadn't looked. I saw a glass wall with an automatic door in the center. I walked closer, there was no sign. A woman walked through the door and I peeked in behind her and saw more than fifty ticket counters. Bingo. The ticket office.

There is a remarkable absence of signage in Turkey.

The bus system is confusing because there are so many different companies. I'm not sure if one is better than another or how to compare experiences, reliability or prices. I walked up to a ticket office that said, "Isparta" and bought a ticket.

When they reserve your ticket, they always note whether you are a man or a woman, as Muslim women cannot sit next to a man who is a stranger. I wasn't asked if I wanted an aisle seat or a window seat but having the right ticket in my hand was enough. I wondered how I'd figure out which seat was number 8? I've never noticed numbers on bus seats.

Denizli is an interesting city. If you research things to do here, all the recommendations are to leave the city and go somewhere else. Really. This is a textile city, but most people come for attractions out of town. I found my hotel on a website that noted it was across the street from the bus station, so it would be easy to get out of the city and tour the notable places in the area.

After breakfast I returned to my room and slept for hours. When I woke, I drank water and slept again and might have slept away the afternoon if I didn't force myself to get up and out. I always followed the late nights with the family in Selçuk with a few hours of writing before I went to bed. Some nights I fell asleep at the computer, then would wake early, before the family, to finish my writing.

Since I had a good bus station orientation earlier in the day, finding the minibus to Pamukkale was easy. I got one of the last seats and paid less than a dollar for the 20-minute ride.

Pamukkale means "cotton castle" in Turkish and the water park does look like giant mounds of cotton candy. It was formed as volcanic lava dissolved calcium below the earth, and then deposited it along naturally made terraces on the surface, where it hardened into limestone.

The rule here is the opposite of restaurants in the states: no shoes. After paying a large fee, you're instructed to take off your shoes and start climbing the slippery slope.

I walked carefully along the UNESCO World Heritage Site and Eighth Wonder of the World, along the ridges that were at times sharp and at other times slippery and at other times offered an incredibly satisfying foot massage. I kept thinking someone was going to tell me to put my shoes on and stop splashing around in puddles. I waded up to my knees and rubbed the mud into my skin just in case it really did have healing powers, as the ancient Romans believed.

Over five thousand people visit the site every day, so I had lots of company as I trekked up the hill by stepping along the travertines (terraces) and took my time; no need to fall off the white cliff where there was, of course, no railing or signs warning that there was an edge. In fact, there were no billboards or flashing lights or "media noise" of any kind. If it weren't so hot out, I might consider this a good dose of daily exercise.

The bonus for making it to the top of the hill was that #1. you could put your shoes back on, and #2. the ancient city of Hierapolis was there to be (re)discovered at no extra charge. When I thought about visiting ruins, I figured that you'd arrive and have all the buildings in a small area where you might walk around and see them without much effort.

Not so. Hierapolis is scattered along the mountainside with paths leading from one old building to another, and the most interesting things required laborious climbs up steep hills.

I wish someone had recommended sturdy shoes for walking along the ruins; there were a lot of small rocks on the dirt paths. At least I had sandals where most people were stumbling around in flip-flops looking at the remains of baths, temples, monuments and the big theater.

Since I didn't have a renowned archaeologist showing me around Hierapolis, I read the posted signs in English, then made up my own stories. "This building is a municipal building, very old, original." And "This building is where they kept the bad children—no views." And "This used to be a disco where Cleopatra and Marc Antony got down to the pop tunes of the day before their epic video game competition and hotdog-eating contests, so that when they headed to the healing baths, they could truly relax."

I should probably offer tours.

I made my way up the hill to St. Philip's Fountain, a pilgrimage site. Though nobody is sure which Philip is buried here or which Philip people came to pray to, it is commonly believed that this Philip was one of Jesus's apostles and that he was crucified here, upside down, per his wish.

I find it interesting that he was able to direct his crucifixion. These days there's no possibility of directing your demise; oh, how times have changed. Just in case it was the religious leader, I prayed again for the children of the world, that they may have food, shelter, education, safety and be able to live with their families.

I learned that St. Philip was the patron saint of mirth. Hello joy. Rather than rejoicing that I'd found another religious leader from the Bible, I celebrated finding the man responsible for joy. How cool is that? I said a faster, second prayer to St. Philip: And may we all experience joy, daily.

It was nearly dusk; many people were heading down the travertines, so I decided to walk down the road. I'd read that it was three kilometers, under two miles. I figured I could walk that in under a half hour at an end-of-the-day slow pace. At first there was a lot of activity along the road, then it became this desolate, hot walk through the wilderness. Was it safe to wander out there by myself?

Several cars and buses passed. I waved a hello wave.

I walked for a half hour and wasn't anywhere near the town. In fact it looked like I had a lot more than three kilometers left to walk. There was only a half hour of sunlight left in the day. I walked faster. I wasn't afraid of getting lost, but I wasn't keen on being out there in the dark. Hello, phone flashlight.

A car slowed and offered me a ride. I waved it on. But when a second car slowed to offer a ride, I looked at who was in the car: a man driving, his wife wearing a head scarf, and an elderly woman in the back seat also wearing a head scarf.

"Yes. Please," I said. "I'd love a ride."

The whole family waved me to the back passenger door. I climbed in next to the old lady. She was holding two bags of tomatoes of the reddest hue and smiled a big, mostly toothless smile. I put my hand on my heart, bowed my head slightly and returned the smile.

She brought her hands to her heart and as the car drove down the mountain, this sweet woman and I locked eyes and smiled at each other.

In broken English the driver asked where I was from. I should have said, "America" which is what the world calls us, but without thinking I said "New York."

He and his wife talked to each other in Turkish for a while, then he said to me, "That a new place?"

I nodded. "Yes. A new place."

We rode down the hill as their GPS called out the turns in Turkish.

We'd been driving for over five minutes when I saw a sign that said three more kilometers until we reached the town.

At the bottom of the hill I got out of the car, thanked them profusely and gave one last smile to the old woman who reached out her hand, not to shake but to touch. I held her hand for a moment, smiled, touched my heart then called out repeating thanks as I closed the door.

As I walked into town to find the minibus back to Denizli, I thought about how many good people there are in the world. I know, the inverse is true too, but there are so many good people in this world. And there are many good people in Turkey, and I am good at finding these good people and cherishing our time together.

A tombstone in the Denizli cemetery demonstrating that Turkish was not always the language of Turkey.

DAY 17: DENIZLI: DEMONSTRATION

This morning at breakfast, a Turkish woman walked up to my table and put her hand on the back of a chair.

I nodded, signaling that she could sit at my table. She was well dressed and carrying a Louis Vuitton bag. She could not speak English. She set her backpack and purse on the chair and then headed to the breakfast buffet.

I thought about how trusting she was, leaving her bag and her backpack on the chair and then turning her back on them. I carry my bag everywhere since it has my passport and my money. What kind of person leaves her bags unattended?

Then I got that creepy feeling. What if...what if she had planted something at my table? A bomb? A gun? It's one of the rules of travel, don't let anyone leave any packages near you.

I tried to put a nonchalant look on my face as I watched her choose her breakfast. If she left the room, I'd leave the room, too. Fast. Without explanation.

Moments later she returned to my table, sat down, and ate her breakfast of bread and eggs. (She took no olives and no cheese. Is she Turkish?)

It's the kind of thing you must think about when you're traveling in a country with active terrorism. Two days ago, two children in a different part of Turkey were killed by a terrorist group that planted new roadside bombs. Today Turkey led airstrikes against Iraq, a neighboring country.

A taxi driver told me that the president of my country, Mr. Trump as he called him, had been ordering killing sprees in Syria, another neighboring country, for two years.

The driver talked to me over his shoulder as he drove. "If he kills Muslims, then he kills my brother."

I had looked at him, quizzically.

He'd nodded. "We know Americans don't know about the American killings in Syria."

I knew very little about what was happening in Syria. I knew there was unrest. I knew there were many, many refugees, but I had no idea that my country was actively policing that part of the world.

Normally when I travel, I'm careful to learn the history of the country I'm visiting. Clearly that wasn't enough. I should have paid attention to what was going on in the surrounding countries, too.

I looked at him blankly.

He shrugged. "We think it will take five years before Americans know the truth about your president murdering the Syrians."

These things were on my mind as I finished my breakfast and got ready to wander around the city.

There are four things I check for before I head out exploring: notebook, phone, sunglasses and water. I was ready. I pulled on a long-sleeved white shirt over my sleeveless shirt for sun protection.

I heard something outside on the street. Horns beeping. Voices. What was that?

The chanting was in Turkish, so I had no idea what the topic might be. One person led the chant, many repeated it. I looked out the window but didn't see anything. It got louder. The chanting sounded angry.

What was going on? I closed the window, closed the curtains, and sat on the bed. It was a group of people, all shouting. Could it be a high school soccer team selling candies, or a group of kids celebrating...something.

Years ago my friend Mark was working in Egypt and Skyped me on my phone. He greeted me with a slow voice, as if he were underwater. I could hear the ice cubes in his drink click together as he drank something.

"You okay?" I asked.

He sighed. "I did something stupid today. Something really stupid."

He told me the story, slowly, as he replenished his drink. It was a sunny day, and he'd looked out of his hotel window in Cairo and noticed that the traffic had stopped.

He thought it must be a national holiday and thought he should go outside to check it out. The doorman of his hotel tried to stop him, but he laughed at the guy, thinking that this could be a cultural experience, the kind that he could tell me about later.

The people were walking in one direction, almost like a parade without floats. He followed them. They walked together, Mark and the Egyptians, and ended up at an anti-American demonstration where they were burning the American flag, shouting threats to Americans and starting to riot and loot.

He told the story of finding his way to safety, feeling grateful that his mother and father had gifted him with a Mediterranean complexion, he looked European.

When he got to his hotel, it was surrounded by military tanks. They wouldn't let him in.

"I found the guy with the most expensive sunglasses and showed him my passport," Mark said.

The guy was furious that Mark was out on the street, but discreetly got him back to the hotel.

We were both quiet as we let the fear and panic of the day settle down. Then he reminded us both, "If there is ever something going on outside, you stay inside."

I remembered this lesson years later. Clearly there was something going on outside my hotel here in this little city in Turkey. I would stay inside.

I surfed the internet on my phone for a while, then wrote for a while. By one o'clock I hadn't heard anything for a few hours, so I went out.

My first stop was the city cemetery, about a 30-minute walk. I wanted to see old tombstones for proof that there were many different languages spoken in Turkey during the many different occupations over the years.

The cemetery was in the center of the city. The tombstones sat on tended grounds and were shaded by many trees. Shade! I walked up a dirt path, enjoying the variety of tombstones around me.

I easily found headstones written in Arabic and other stones that were so old you couldn't read anything.

I wandered for a while, taking photos and wondering what year the tombstones were from. According to something I read, there are some notable tombs in this cemetery, but I didn't care to search for them.

I left and followed the GPS on my phone to the Old Quarter of Denizli. There weren't many people wandering around, which made me sad for the shops. Too bad I couldn't buy something; there is no room to take trinkets home in my suitcase.

I bought a bottle of water and the seller asked me if I wanted a piece of cheese, or that's what I thought she might have said. She was slicing a big hunk of my favorite soft cheese. Since I wasn't sure if that's what she said, I declined.

At around five o'clock it started raining, hard. I decided to dry off at the hotel before I chose my dinner for tonight. Kebab again?

I reorganized my purse, filled my water bottle from a larger bottle and turned on the air conditioner. The rain stopped and I jumped off the bed, slung my purse over one shoulder and grabbed my sunglasses.

But as I walked towards the door, I heard the chanting again. Many voices. Shouting together. Cheering. Whistling. I wished I knew what they were saying. It got loud enough that I thought I would record their voices so I could ask one of my Turkish friends to translate it for me.

Before I came to Turkey, I did a little research on their political system and found that its policies didn't always reflect being a democratic society. I never asked my new Turkish friends about their views on politics, fearing that either of us would suffer the wrath of some Turkish people who don't think it's a good idea to have opinions about politics.

I met some men who were engineers and taking their city (not Denizli where I was currently) to court for having placed a tax on water that would make water too expensive for people to have in their homes. This city was turning off water for anyone who hadn't paid the enormous fee. The men felt certain that they would win in court, but not certain if they could affect change.

I went online and checked the local newspaper, and translated the page to English with a click from my translations program. There was no mention of a major sporting event or a local rally or a riot.

I wanted to record the chanting from my balcony; I couldn't see the demonstrators, but I could hear them. As soon as I was ready to hit the record button, the Call to Prayers started and the chanting stopped.

It amazed me how respectful people were when the Call to Prayer starts. Music in venues stops. Children quiet. And here, the demonstration stopped, too.

I had a bus ticket out of here first thing in the morning. Good timing.

I put my purse on the bed, kicked off my shoes and decided to stay in. The hotel had a restaurant, but I didn't feel like translating a menu. Luckily, I had some snacks. Almonds for dinner, again.

The noise got progressively louder and angrier. Crowds of people ran through the streets chanting, yelling, beeping car horns and shouting.

It sounded like chaos. They sounded angry. I heard what sounded like gunshots and what sounded like little explosions.

In my room I was removed from what was happening, but the only thing that kept me from the epicenter of the demonstrations was a mob of angry people. Would they come closer? Would they enter my hotel?

I didn't know what the demonstrations were about. Were they protesting low wages as they did several months ago? Were they making a statement about Turkey's political arena or the terrorism that plagues them? Were they upset with America; could I be targeted?

I wanted to know how I fit into their rage.

The crowds grew louder and angrier. I couldn't see them out my window, but they were close by; I could hear them clearly. Were they drinking alcohol? Would this demonstration turn into a riot? I didn't know how to be safe in a place where I couldn't come up with an escape plan.

What if the city shut down from the riots? What if my bus was cancelled? I had no alternative plan.

Years ago a friend lived in Los Angeles during a time when there were riots that passed within a block of her apartment. It terrified her, not knowing which way the crowd would turn. At the time I didn't understand why she was afraid since nobody was clubbing down her door or throwing things through her windows. Today I understood her panic.

I shivered even though it wasn't cold in my hotel room.

I packed my bags, rearranging things so if I had to leave quickly, my purse had everything I needed. I climbed into bed in my clothes; I didn't like the idea of having to evacuate in my pajamas should there be a fire...or something.

If I understood what they were shouting, it might have been an easier night. But something in the not understanding the context made the terror inside me grow with their shouting.

By 1:00 AM the protesting was so loud that when I spoke out loud, "Okay, this needs to stop," I couldn't hear my voice. It sounded like they were on my balcony. They weren't. When I looked out my window, I couldn't see them.

It sounded like more people had joined their movement. Yelling together the same phrases over and over. Horns beeping. Sounds of little explosions. I was too tense to record the noise around me, worried that someone would notice me making a recording and retaliate.

I curled up in bed and reminded myself to breathe. It's no surprise that there's unrest in other places in the world, but this was real, and it was now, and I no longer felt safe.

If there were a tunnel from that hotel room to New York, I would have crawled home. Given in. Finished with this experiment in discovering other parts of the world. I felt alone and wondered why I have repeatedly refused to live a normal life, a safe life of inviting neighbors over for a barbecue and traveling to Florida in the winter to thaw out.

By traveling as far away as I possibly could, was I daring the world to scare me?

The Librarian (on right) and her sister sitting on a bench that looks like a book.

The sisters' father introduces Holly winter Huppert to his herd of goats in Atabey.

DAY 18: ATABEY: KNOTS

I awoke to the first Call to Prayer at 4:50 AM. It was quiet outside. The demonstrations had stopped.

I wondered if anything had changed overnight. Was there someone new in power? Had there been grand-scale arrests? Were those gunshots directed at people or up in the air?

I dressed, finished packing and then went down to breakfast. Two policemen lined up for the buffet behind me. Were they invited because there was extra security needed at breakfast? They sat at a table under the windows.

Nobody stared at me. Nobody moved away from me. One woman who was wearing a head scarf smiled at me and bowed her head. I returned the gestures and ate quietly.

At 8:30 I checked out of the hotel, deciding not to ask about the unrest from the night before. I reluctantly walked outside. What if it wasn't over? What if a bunch of angry people were looking for...trouble?

The streets were quiet. People walked as if they were on their way somewhere.

I walked across the street. It was easy to find the bus to Isparta, after my long study of the building a few days earlier, but I decided to swing by the ticket office—just to be sure I had everything I needed.

A man walked up to me and insisted that he would help me find the ticket office.

"No," I said. "Go away."

I walked quickly, pulling my suitcase behind me, and walked through the automatic doors. Had this scammer offered his help the day before when I was searching, I might have fallen for it, but I'd already bought my ticket.

The counter was right there, across the room. The man who sold me a ticket yesterday watched me approach, but the manipulating slug wouldn't go away. He hovered around me like a mosquito waiting to strike.

I said in a loud voice, "Go away now."

He said, "First you pay, I help. I show you ticket office. Fifty lira."

I stared at him and dropped my voice. I'd barely slept because of the noise on the streets outside my hotel. I was tired and still tense. I said even louder, "Go away now."

He raised his voice, "I call police. You pay me."

I stared him in the eye, pointed at his chest and yelled, "Police! Police! I need the police!"

It's an old travel trick and works in every country. Start yelling, anything, and if you're in a crowded place where others aren't yelling, the police might run to your side, but more importantly the people around you will pay attention.

(Unless you're in New York City. Yelling doesn't work there.)

It was impressive the way my voice echoed through the ticket center.

The man ran away before the police heard my plea.

The men at the ticket counter waved me closer. "He is bad man," they said.

Yeah. Bad man.

Got it.

They directed me to my bus and I guessed which seat was number 8 and prepared to move if anyone knew better. Whenever a bus attendant came near me, I handed him my ticket. After a while the bus pulled out of the station to begin the two-and-a-half-hour journey.

I was relieved to leave Denizli and that long night behind me.

While on the bus, a friend email me from home and said she found the cause of the demonstration online: a young woman—a teacher—had been wrongly jailed several years ago after a major uprising. Though the woman took no part in the uprising, she was imprisoned, as were many innocent people.

Yesterday word got out that the young woman committed suicide in her cell. Her two young children lost their mother, the city lost a teacher and for the rest of us humanity itself seemed cruel.

After a sleepless night, the tragedy of politics weighed heavily on me. How could... Why? Shouldn't... If only....

The librarian who hosted the international breakfast and her sister met my bus with open arms and big smiles. It was a great relief to know someone and once again be welcomed as a guest.

I met the librarian's daughter, a beautiful 14-year-old girl, and the sister's son, a cute 12-year-old boy. We got into the car and started a day of touring around Isparta, a city known for its roses.

They took me to the carpet museum where everything inside had to do with the history of that industry in Turkey: twelve floors of carpet history. Imagine carpets of every size and color hanging from the walls and piled on the floors. The evil-eye emblem was woven into many designs. I learned that the thinner carpets were more valuable, as were carpets with the most knots.

It was interesting that on a day that I was a bit "knotted" up myself, I was learning about knots.

After lunch in Eğirdir where we enjoyed views of the largest lake in this part of Turkey, the sisters and I sat by the water and breathed in the clean air. It was a beautiful day, sunny, windy, warm. We drove on to the other side of the lake and went to a little zoo. The first exhibit had stray cats enclosed in an exhibit. None of us understood the meaning, why were the stray cats locked inside?

The sisters and I walked around for a while, the kids were tired and decided to wait near the car where they could play on their phones.

We sat on benches that looked like poetry books and a friendly man insisted that we share his sunflower seeds with him.

I never would have accepted food from a stranger, but the sisters did; I followed their lead. We put the shells into our mouths, one at a time, cracked them open and picked out the tiny morsel of a seed to eat. Delicious.

After a while he asked if we would prefer coffee or tea. We each placed our order and he left to buy the drinks. In the states I never would let a stranger buy my drink and carry it to me. What if he put some drug inside? The women weren't worried.

We sipped our drinks and talked to the man and found out he was a primary school teacher in Antalya. The sisters were both high school English teachers. Here we were, four teachers sitting together, drinking hot drinks on a hot summer day in a small city in rural Turkey.

We stopped for ice cream along the highway at a shop with long lines. Since we were in Isparta, where roses are plentiful, I decided to try the rose ice cream. Sweet. Cold. Creamy. Rose. For the first time in years, lemon took a back seat and rose moved to the front of the line. I'm not sure if rose ice cream would be as good back home, but I'm going to eat as much of it as I can at Irfando's place in these next few days.

I talked to the sisters about my long night, and one sister looked online and said she couldn't find any mention of it. I asked them if they were afraid because tensions between Iraq and Turkey were escalating. The librarian said that there were always things going on in their country and that they'd learned to let the government worry about the problems.

We drove to their widowed father's house, which was their childhood home, in Atabey, which is about a 15-minute drive from Isparta. He's lived there for over forty years. It's a bright house with enough beds and couches for us all to sleep. The librarian pointed to the carpet on the floor in my room and told me her grandmother made it over eighty years ago.

"But it looks new," I said. "It looks like it was made this year."

The librarian said, "We send it to a cleaner every few years," as if the cleaner made the carpet appear younger.

I asked if there were any more handmade carpets in the house and she pointed to an extra-large red rug in the living room. She said her mother made it as her dowry when she was 17 years old.

It was a masterpiece. A deep red color. Precise detailing. Zero wear. The colors strong. It was a thin carpet.

I said, "This one needs to be hanging in that museum."

How could a carpet that old look so new? To think a carpet could last longer than the weaver's life and will continue to decorate the homes of this same family through many more generations is incredible.

The sisters were worried about inviting me to their father's house, thinking it was too simple a place for me to feel at home, but I found his house to be more than comfortable. I had my own room with enough space to unpack a little. There were two bathrooms and only one of them had a squat toilet: I was happy.

The kitchen lacked enough chairs for us all to sit together; I'd happily stand to eat for the gift of being here with the family.

After dinner we walked to a nearby park and I let the sisters look through the photographs on my phone. My house. My kindergarten classroom. My family. My dates. My creek. They asked about one photo on a beach and I told them I had taken a trip to California last spring.

The sister said, "There are many songs about California."

I asked which ones she knew, and the three of us walked home singing along to "Hotel California" from a YouTube video on her phone.

I felt honored to be invited to this oasis of family. And in the quiet of this small and loving community, I slowly let go of where I was last night and settled into this night. Be present. This is where I am now. I am safe.

The video changed and we sang a round of "California Dreaming" as we walked down the middle of the road to my home for the night. I agreed with the song: it would be safer to stay home, but I continue to choose the excitement of the road.

The sisters' cousin shows off her shirt with English words that read, "Chillin' with my Snowmies."

A beggar approached while the sisters and Holly Winter Huppert were drinking tea. The sisters each gave him money and when he demanded more more money, they gave him more.

A woman at the market in Atabey selling milk in recycled soda bottles.

Weighing vegetables at the market in Atabey.

A beautiful wedding in Atabey.

Holly Winter Huppert poses with the sisters' mother's cousin
after the wedding luncheon.

DAY 19: ATABEY: WEDDING

I asked, "Is what I'm wearing okay?" I had on a pair of green capri pants, a black sleeveless blouse and sandals.

"Yes," said the librarian.

Her sister added, "You look beautiful."

They were speaking English, but I didn't understand. I said, "But we are going to a wedding, so I should wear better clothes."

"No," the sisters said.

The librarian said, "It's only a wedding lunch."

I was in a small town in Turkey. There were no condos here or even apartment complexes. Most people had lived here in the same small house their whole lives; everyone knew everybody else. The friends I was staying with for a few days grew up here in Atabey, then each sister made her life in a different part of the country. The sisters met in this small mountain town each summer to spend time with their elderly father.

I said, "In my country if you go to a wedding, you wear fancy clothes."

"Not here," the sister said.

Both sisters were high school English teachers, so we didn't need to use a translation program to communicate.

I said, "It's not a problem if I wear a black shirt?"

The librarian said, "No problem. We go now."

We drove for a few minutes then stopped to offer a ride to their mother's elderly cousin, who was walking. The cousin was a short, elderly woman who wore long sleeves, long pants and had her head covered. Though it was nearly ninety degrees, she wore a light sweater over her clothes. I felt like I might faint from heat exhaustion from just looking at her.

I posed for a photograph with the cousin when we arrived, and she said something to me in Turkish. The librarian said that she gave me a blessing in Turkish, but that she didn't know how to translate it.

I bowed my head and smiled at the cousin, thanking her for her kind words.

We arrived at the luncheon. I was worried that the bride and groom would think I was an interloper who had come for a free meal.

The librarian said, again, "You sure you don't mind sharing one dish? We will all eat from one dish."

"I'm sure."

There was an area with large, round wooden tables and plastic chairs and there was a tarp to keep the tables shaded. Many people were already eating. At first, I worried that we were late, then I noticed that it was more of an "open house" style, people were coming and going.

We sat and helped ourselves to a cold-water cup (a disposable cup with a peel-off lid.) Someone brought us each a large spoon and then placed one bowl of rice soup on our table. We each picked up our own spoon and began eating from the same dish, like you might do if you were eating from a fondue pot. We each spooned soup from our side of the bowl into our mouths, then reached in for more. I tried to get extra tomato sauce onto my spoon; the spice made the soup even better.

What a relief to be around the sisters, who had checked the menu and could tell me what was gluten-free, a necessity in my diet.

I'd had several tastes when the librarian asked me if I liked it.

I smiled a bigger smile, nodded and ate more.

When we finished, the young man serving our table brought the meat and rice dish, a bean dish and pickled vegetables. We ate and talked, and I met other relatives who were also at the luncheon.

As I greeted one relative, the woman said something to me. The sisters laughed and told me that the woman said I was skinny. This had happened several times since I'd been in Turkey. I smiled and thanked her, not sure how to respond to someone discussing my weight. Someone else greeted me the same way; I smiled and thanked her, too.

The sisters laughed and translated, "She thought all Americans were fat."

I laughed. "Many are."

~

Wedding Luncheon in Atabey:
Course 1: Rice Soup (*Pirinç Çorbası*)
Course 2: Rice with Lamb (*Kabune*)
Beans (*Nohut*)
Pickled Vegetables (*Tursu*)
Course 3: Dessert (*Helva*)

~

A young woman with brown hair, the bride's sister, welcomed me through her husband who spoke great English and asked us to come to the ceremony tonight. We said we would be there. I hoped that they weren't just being polite by extending the invitation to me, since I've never met the bride or the groom. In the States, a bride would not be happy to have last-minute additions to her carefully planned party.

I asked the sisters about a movement some people make when greeting each other.

"A movement?" the librarian asked.

"You take the hand of the person you are greeting, kiss the back of his or her hand and then touch it to your forehead."

"Ooh. Yes," the sisters said together.

They explained that this was a sign of great respect. You greet an older relative from an older generation in a different way. Rather than kissing each cheek, you say hello while looking him or her in the eye. Then you hold his or her right hand, kiss the back of his or her hand and then touch that kiss to your forehead.

I asked them many questions.

"It is our way," the sister said.

After lunch we went to a cousin's house for tea, which might be the national pastime in Turkey. Earlier in the day when we stopped for tea, again, I joked that we hadn't had tea for a whole hour, so I could see that it was time for more.

At home in New York I drink zero caffeine in a day or risk not being able to sleep at night. Here I was up to two glasses a day of their Turkish tea, which I thought was a giant leap, although tea is served in those small tulip-shaped glass cups that only hold a quarter cup of liquid at a time. So I was priding myself on being able to drink literally a half cup of tea each day.

It was considered rude to refuse a cup of tea, but I learned to refuse tea all day long. I wouldn't be able to sleep if I drank so much caffeine, and when I don't sleep, life becomes far more difficult, so I learned to refuse in the nicest ways I could think of.

Nobody seemed to mind. In Selçuk, the archaeologist's wife bought me herbal tea to drink and said it was no problem for me to drink something different.

I loved the way people here drink tea or Turkish coffee. They sit down, no matter how rushed they are to get somewhere. They sit and sip, never carrying a drink on the go.

A woman at that international breakfast told the story of a Turkish man who was moving to America and in order to prepare himself, he got a metal drink container and carried his coffee around with him, like an American would.

Yes, that's my cultural norm, rush around while sipping a hot drink.

We returned to their father's house for a rest. I slept for hours; it was so peaceful in the country where I could hear the birds singing.

Several family members came to visit, an aunt and uncle, and a brother and sister-in-law.

The sisters nodded towards their aunt who was much older, and I watched as the sisters' brother greeted her. He looked into her eyes and said hello, then he held her right hand, kissed the back of it and held her hand to his forehead for a long moment.

I looked at the sisters with wide eyes while they smiled back at me. Now I understood.

The librarian whispered to me, "Do you want me to ask my brother to greet her again, so you can get a picture?"

"No, thank you," I said quickly, not wanting to disrupt the greeting.

I watched the sister prepare Turkish coffee. The coffee powder is ground as fine as cocoa powder, which makes a thick cup of coffee. The sister spooned some coffee powder into an open kettle and waited for it to reach a hard boil. She placed small handled cups that held half of a measured cup on a tray, poured a little coffee into each one, then added a little more.

I asked her why she didn't just fill each cup before filling the next cup. She said that by adding the coffee in small bits, there were more bubbles. People here like bubbles. I never saw anyone add any milk to their coffee or tea, but many add sugar to their tea.

The sister's uncle asked me a question in Turkish.

The librarian translated, "He wants to know if you like Turkey."

"Very much," I smiled.

He said something else to the sisters. The librarian translated. "He said you must be living a good life, to be here with us."

It was one of my biggest surprises in traveling here. At home the older generation might be suspicious of a lone traveler; not here. Here they believed that if you were spending time with them, it was for all the right reasons, as if God orchestrated the event.

I shared a similar view, that good things happen to good people, but had never applied it to myself and my travels before now.

The aunt and uncle shared dried mulberries with us and after I'd eaten a few they asked, through the sisters, if I liked them.

"Very much." I smiled and ate another.

With that everyone stood up. "We go now," the librarian said. "We will get mulberries."

It seemed like an abrupt ending to our visit.

I've noticed that I must be careful in saying that I like anything in this country, because people are so generous that if I show favor to anything, they will gift me with more. I worried the aunt and uncle were going to gift me with a gallon of dried mulberries, since I liked them so much. How would I carry them with me?

I grabbed my day bag and we drove to a house about five minutes away.

It was like something out of a Disney movie. You like mulberries? Then, snap of fingers, here you go: two giant mulberry trees at the peak of ripeness.

You have to admit, I say that I like mulberries, and then it just happens to be mulberry season in this very neighborhood where I am staying. Fantastical, amiright?

We climbed to the upper terrace at a different aunt's house and we were all encouraged to eat as many berries as we could. They'd already picked and stored as many as they could eat. The aunt's husband had planted the mulberry trees fifty years ago when he was a boy.

White mulberries. Large. Juicy. Sweet. Addictive. I picked and ate happily. The uncle filled his hands with the best possible berries, then poured them into my hands. I ate and ate. He gifted me with another handful and another and another. I was so full I couldn't eat more, but I did.

Next, we drove to this same aunt and uncle's house and the uncle encouraged me to pick a mini-cucumber from his garden so I could eat it.

The sisters laughed. "How do you say it in Turkish?"

It was one of my words. "Salatalik."

The sisters corrected my pronunciation.

Inside the house the aunt had prepared some more food for us to eat. There was a large round tray that was placed on a small table. We sat on short stools with our knees practically touching the tray and ate from it. Any seeds or pits or cores from the fruit were left on the tray. Under the tray was a giant sheet, so if we dropped something, it would not ruin the carpet.

This must be one of the secrets for how they keep their carpets looking like new. They protect them when there is food around.

I sighed slowly, completely full. The aunt was worried that I wasn't eating enough, so she sliced a small pear and handed me half.

I know. I know. I said thank you, and ate more.

The librarian showed me the handmade carpets around us. The uncle designs them, and the aunt makes them. Sometimes the uncle helps, and they knot the carpets together.

The carpets were colorful with fun designs, and I was in awe of the great skill used in making them.

I asked the sister, "Are all Turkish men so helpful? I noticed the archaeologist I stayed with helped a lot around the house, too."

She shrugged. "Some are. Some aren't."

Outside her uncle's house, I went to put on my shoes and noticed that our shoes were pointed away from the door.

The librarian noticed my hesitation. "What do you see?"

"The shoes are different," I said.

"Yes." She nodded her head fast, then explained that when you visit someone's house, while you are inside visiting, the hostess will sneak back outside and turn the shoes so that they are pointing away from the door.

It is a sign of respect and makes it easier to put your shoes on.

It was the first time I'd noticed this, and I vowed to pay more attention: how many hostesses had done this during my travels so far?

We returned to their father's house with the brother and his wife because, sigh, it was dinnertime. I was sure I couldn't eat another bite, but these were the eggplants we had bought at the market that afternoon.

"When did you cook this?" I asked.

The librarian said, "When you were napping. My sister wanted you to have a very good dinner."

I had only agreed to take a rest because I thought the sisters were resting, too. They tricked me into napping.

I was raised in a family where if someone cooked for two hours and made a spectacular dinner while you napped, then you must eat two servings. I couldn't meet that standard, but I could eat a small helping of the roasted eggplant. Delicious. Delicious. What was that spice?

Nutritionists have touted the Mediterranean diet as being one of the healthiest ways to eat. On my trip I noticed that Turkish people eat remarkably little protein. When I ate breakfast with the family in

Selçuk, all four of us would share one egg, or one link of sausage. Many meals had no meat or protein at all other than the yogurt dripped over the food.

I didn't miss the meat; the vegetables were diverse and interesting, and I happily ate as many vegetables as I could for all three meals.

After the trip, when I'd read about the Mediterranean diet, I'd think about what I saw: four vegetables to one protein, where one serving of protein might be closer to one or two ounces, once a day, plus yogurt at every meal.

We got ready to go to the wedding. I asked the sisters if I should change my clothes.

"Why would you do that?" the librarian asked.

I said, "Because we are going to the wedding ceremony."

I know, we had this same exchange earlier. But was there never a time to spiffy up for a wedding?

We walked down the road towards the loud music. We arrived during the ceremony and found chairs along the outer ring of seated people. The bride and groom said their I do's, or yeses, and went right from the ceremony to the first dance.

Her dress was a perfect bell shape with a hint of sparkle. She and the groom smiled big smiles as they danced. Women danced around the bride and men danced around the groom. The bride's sister invited me to join the dance around the bride. The sister joined me, and I followed in her footsteps.

Arms out, step, small step. Step, small step. My smile might have been bigger than the bride's because I couldn't believe I was here, in a remote town in Turkey, dancing at a wedding. We circled the bride and danced some more.

One of the groomsmen found me later. He handed me a pin with fake money, a promise of prosperity, and motioned for me to help him.

"It's okay," the librarian said. "He is the best friend of the groom."

When it was our turn, the best friend pointed to the groom's sash and I pinned the money pendant on. The bride and groom smiled at each other as I helped set their marriage's good luck.

The best friend motioned for me to repeat a phrase in Turkish. He said the phrase, slowly, but I couldn't hold on to a single word. I asked to hear the phrase again, as if this were a game show. Nope. Still couldn't repeat the phrase. So he said a few words that I did my best to repeat. The newlyweds laughed at my mispronunciation.

The groomsman looked his best friend in the eye and said the phrase again. He spoke it twice, once to the right and once to the left. The friends looked at each other for a long moment while the groom accepted the words, then the groom nodded.

I said to the new husband and wife, using the simplest words I could think of, "You look beautiful. Have a beautiful life. Many, many blessings."

They smiled at each other, then smiled at me. The bride, another English teacher, said "Thank you."

I danced some more in the Turkish style to the Turkish music and the sister always tagged along, dancing next to me, so she could translate and answer questions at this community celebration where everyone was encouraged to come as you are.

Eating a snack at the aunt's and uncle's house.

The uncle and aunt show off their latest carpets. He designs them, she makes them. Sometimes he helps make them, too. The S is for her name, Saniye and the I is for his name, Ismail.

DAY 20: ANTALYA: SPLURGE

I n the morning, the sisters and I migrated to the kitchen to make breakfast. It was my last morning with my friends and I was feeling sad about leaving.

The librarian washed some eggs. "These are boiled eggs."

Wanting to help put breakfast on the table, I picked up an egg and was about to bump it against the counter so I could peel it when the librarian started waving her hands in front of her as fast as she could.

She shouted, "THESE WILL BE BOILED EGGS."

We laughed and laughed at this perfect demonstration of using those pesky verb tenses: hello, future tense.

Teaching English at this stop, to the sisters and their children, was a different experience because the sisters are English teachers at the high school level. Rather than pointing to objects and naming them, I tried to help them go deeper.

When they were looking at photographs on my phone, I showed them a picture I took of a bunch of ducks swimming in a row. I told them the saying, "All of my ducks are in a row." We'd practice it on and off as they fought to get the prepositions correct.

We'd passed a restaurant called the Big Apple. "That's the

nickname for New York," I said. "And if you love someone you can say, 'You are the apple of my eye.'"

Although the sisters use fun and games to teach English in their schools, many programs in Turkey base their language learnings on complicated grammar lessons, so the sisters' children were reluctant to talk to me. Was I the Grammar Police sent to haunt them on their summer holidays?

But when I pulled out a deck of cards, the kids were willing to play.

We started with the game, War, the irony of which was not lost on me. It was an easy game to teach: we each put down a card, highest card wins—meaning if the librarian put down a nine and it is the highest face value on every card put down in this round, then she gets to collect all of our cards and add them to her pile of cards.

The kids loved the game. We played for a long time. I lost almost immediately because I was the first one to run out of cards, which proves that I am not a card shark.

Next, I taught them the game, Go Fish, which sneakily required the kids to use their English skills. The object of the game is to make as many matches as you can. Each of us held five cards, and when it was your turn you had to ask the person next to you, "Do you have a four?" The person would have to respond, "No. I do not have a four. Go fish." And the asker could pick up a card from the upside-down pile on the table in hopes of making a match. Or the person you are asking can say, "Yes. I have a four. Here it is."

I lost this game, too, which proves that I might be a winner when it comes to travel, but not when it comes to cards.

In their excitement the kids kept trying to switch languages. Um, sorry, no Turkish at my English lessons.

The boy wanted to teach the next game. His embarrassment in speaking a second language changed to frustration in finding the right words to explain himself.

It was a bluffing game where you placed cards or matches face down on the table in a central pile and stated what the cards were. "I'm putting down two threes." Anyone in the group could challenge you. If you're caught in a lie, you must pick up all the cards. If you're caught in a truth, the challenger must pick up the cards. The one who runs out of cards first wins.

I put down a pair of kings which was a good hand. To spice up the game, I pretended that the cards I put down made me nervous. I dipped my head low and looked around the group quickly and ran my hand through my hair several times, as if I couldn't sit still. This was like a backwards bluff.

The boy challenged me and had to pick up the entire stack of cards.

"But you look bluff," he said.

I shrugged. Teachers excel at bluffing.

While we were eating breakfast there was a squeal from the other room. I thought the daughter was still sleeping. Mouse? Mosquito? Spilled nail polish?

Her mother ran in to check and came back with tears in her eyes. "She just heard about her exam to get into high school. We have waited so long."

In Turkey, all students must take competitive exams before they start high school. Their score will determine what school they can attend. Each school is rated on a continuum. Her dream high school required a dreamy high score on the exam. Though she had taken it a while ago, they had to wait months for the results.

The librarian returned to the kitchen and stood in the doorway with her hands on her cheeks. "She got into her school."

We all cheered and laughed and hugged.

The girl checked in with her friends, one after the other. While we ate breakfast, she regaled us with live updates.

Her best friend got into her school, too. Another friend made it. Oh, but one didn't make it. The daughter called the friend who didn't make it and they cried together on the phone.

The librarian started calling her friends to share the good news while the sister and I washed the dishes from breakfast. At this house they put a basin with hot soapy water on the counter to wash the dishes. The sink is used to rinse.

The sisters took me to see their mother's grave and I helped them clean it off. They decided to return later to scrub it clean and plant some new flowers around it.

We drove to their father's goat farm, which I had asked to see. He met us there and opened a large gate. Inside was a courtyard surrounded by a high cement wall. One end of the yard had a shaded area, under which a herd of goats relaxed in the shade. This whole compound was for raising goats.

Their father walked to the goats and they all stepped out to greet him. He turned and looked at me, and as if on cue, the goats looked at me, too. I took a photograph, which the sisters would later say was the best picture of their father that they had. I was happy to share it with them.

The sisters translated for me when I told him that my mother had goats, too.

He made a cutting motion with his hand.

I knew what he was asking. Does she kill the goats and eat them? I shook my head, "No. She doesn't eat them."

He rolled his eyes as if I were wasting his time and turned back to his flock.

On the way home we stopped by the bazaar so the sisters could buy their food for the next few days. This "farmer's market" was so much louder than the one in Selçuk. The vendors called out what they were selling, and the voices of people buying added to a happy din of a community supporting each other: buying, selling, greeting.

The sisters greeted various friends and family who were also shopping. I started losing track of who people were—it's especially difficult to recognize women who didn't wear a head scarf when we visited them at home but are wearing one in public. And even the women who wore a head scarf at our first meeting had different scarves on for this meeting. I have trouble greeting people when they are out of place, but this was extra difficult.

It didn't matter. I greeted every person as if I'd already met them: "Hello, friendly people."

We returned to the house, where I packed and we loaded the car with my stuff.

When it was time to say goodbye, the father became serious and spoke Turkish to the librarian.

She translated, "He said that next summer there will be an important wedding in the family, and he would like to formally invite you to attend."

I said, "Ask him if there will be fresh goat to eat at the party. If there is fresh goat, I will be there."

The sisters translated my question, would there be goat at the wedding?

He got tears in his eyes, and nodded his head in the affirmative and insisted that I stay longer next year.

It was difficult to leave these lovely people, but if I wanted to see more of Turkey, I had to move on. The sisters and their children drove me to Isparta.

We parked and the boy "drove" my suitcase behind us. The librarian asked a man about the bus to Antalya, and he pointed to a bus backing out of the spot next to us. The driver understood the international sign of the point and pulled the bus back into the space.

We hugged fast and hard and I said thank you again and again. The luggage attendant took my suitcase and put it under with the luggage. We hurried our goodbyes, but it takes a while to kiss each person on two cheeks and then look them in the eye and thank them again.

My friends ushered me to the door of the bus. The driver pointed to the front seat, telling me to sit there.

Okay. I can sit there.

The sister shouted to me, "Are you okay?"

"Yes," I said. "But tell him I don't have a ticket." I was losing my translators.

The sister yelled to the driver in rapid Turkish.

The driver nodded an annoyed look that said, "Obviously she doesn't have a ticket."

My friends waved to me for a long, long time.

I moped during the two-hour ride to my next destination. Leaving never gets easier.

I hadn't done my homework, so when I arrived in Antalya, I didn't have a cheap way to get to my hotel. I checked my phone; the hotel was an hour walk from the bus station, no thanks. I went to the ticket office, but when the door opened I noticed there weren't any signs and I didn't know who to ask and I still didn't speak Turkish and I didn't feel like going through security just to save a few dollars by taking a local bus.

Taxi!

This next hotel was my splurge of the trip. I was gifted with a few hundred dollars and told to find something special for myself as I traveled. I thought a room in the old quarter for two nights would be fitting

Antalya is the start of what is called the Turkish Riviera. When I showed the sisters where I was staying, they said that the old mansion that had been restored to a boutique hotel was the best place in the Old Town.

Score!

The only problem was that my taxi driver had no idea how to get there. He called to someone before he started the meter. I think his mentor might have told him to just start driving. I could visualize the price of the ride tripling as he slowed in front of every hotel in the city, looking for mine.

I pulled up the location on my phone and leaned into the front of the taxi where the driver could see it. Together we decided each turn; if we got lost, we could blame Mr. Google.

The one-way winding streets of the old part of town were not made for a meandering taxi. The driver squeezed the car through openings between buildings that were so tight, I'm pretty sure we only made it through because my sharp inhale made the taxi a little bit smaller. Or something.

The driver's only English was, "No problem" and he said it after every narrow squeeze. I'm always happy to let someone practice learning my native language.

When we were within a few blocks, I bade the driver goodbye. He couldn't figure out which one-way street would lead us to the hotel. He was annoyed that I wouldn't let him drop me off at the door.

The hotel was housed in a beautiful old building where the floors and walls were decorated with mosaics. The courtyard was lush with plants around a small swimming pool. The owner was waiting to check me in. I was going to love it there.

After checking in to my dream room, I plugged in my phone, to be sure it had enough power to use my GPS to find my way back to the hotel, then started wandering, stopping to photograph anything that caught my eye.

Whoever designed this town back in the Ottoman days must have been a rebel who didn't believe in a grid system; this town is as difficult to navigate as Seville, Spain.

I found notable things by accident: Karaalioğlu Park. The Roman Harbor. When I happened upon the Ethnology Museum, I went inside right away, knowing that the chances of finding it again were slim.

Back in my room, I sent some photos to the sisters and let them know I had figured out how to get back to my hotel, and had also figured out where to get the bus to the next place when it was time to leave in two days' time.

The librarian returned my message: "All of your ducks are in a row."

Photo next page: Üçkapılar or Hadrian's Gate was built in 130 AD, in Antalya.

Outside the Hamam in Antalya.

A street in Antalya.

DAY 21: ANTALYA: HAMAM

"Do you have any questions?" the receptionist asked in perfect English as he adjusted his hand over the computer.

This was my first time to a *hamam*, which is also called a Turkish bath. Friends had given me some pointers, but they mostly had to do with loving the experience. I had a lot of questions.

I said, "What do I need to know?"

He said a few things in perfect English. I understood everything he said, but was thinking about a website that warned that a woman should never, ever go to a Turkish bath and get worked on by a man. This bath, which was in the old quarter of Antalya, was just a five-minute walk from my hotel; convenience and more than four hundred excellent reviews on the internet made me override that website's warning.

Was my curiosity about another culture putting me in harm's way?

The receptionist handed me two pieces of cloth and told me to go and change.

I was given a small changing room next to the reception area and a key to lock the door to keep my things safe. I picked up the cloth—it was just a towel. I thought it would be a bathrobe.

I stepped out of the cubicle and said, "I don't know what to do. This is only a towel..."

The receptionist said, "Some people wear bikinis. You can do that, or you can wear nothing. It's up to you."

"I didn't bring a bathing suit," I said. Should I run back to my hotel to get one?

My friend in Selçuk was telling me about what the hamam was like when she mispronounced the word, "bikini." We'd gotten off topic after that conversation. That must be what she was trying to tell me, that you could wear a bathing suit for your treatment.

I returned to my changing room, removed my jewelry and tucked it into my purse. I covered the purse with one of the pieces of cloth and wrapped myself in the other piece. I felt too naked, so I put my underwear and shorts back on then wrapped my upper half in the towel. I stepped back into the reception area.

There are many places to get a Turkish bath, but I liked the idea of having one so close to my hotel. If I waited until I got to Istanbul, I might have to take two subways and a taxi to find a place.

A man appeared and he gestured for me to follow him. I followed him through the 600-year-old building with marble floors and arched ceilings. We ducked through a small door, up two steps, down one step. He walked me across a small, empty room and into another room.

I was the only guest here. I thought Turkish baths were brimming with people. Anything you read about them claims they are a social center.

We entered another room. Hot. Dry air. Different than the hot air outside, but uncomfortable all the same. There was a large marble slab in the center and a series of water taps around the sides of the room.

The man motioned to the giant marble slab and motioned for me to sit on it.

Really?

I sat; he pointed from my back to the slab. He wants me to lie down? Keeping the towel tucked around me, I lay back. The slab was hot. Really hot. I wished I hadn't spent the last hour walking around outside in the hundred-degree heat.

This wasn't relaxing. I was sitting in a giant sauna wrapped in a towel, lying on a hot slab. Wasn't this supposed to be a relaxing day?

The man pointed to my forehead and then to some taps on the wall. He walked over to a tap, mimed filling a plastic bowl with water and pouring it over his head.

Either he was miming that I need to pay attention to when it gets too hot so I can leave, or that if I get too hot, I can pour water over myself. If only there were other people around whom I could watch, so I would know what to do.

The man walked out a small "Hobbit" door next to the spigot and I was alone.

It was hot. Too hot. Uncomfortably hot. I loosened the towel and laid it over me. This is so much hotter than a typical sauna.

I pulled off my shorts and my underwear and put them in my bag of writing supplies I'd brought with me in case there was "down time" and I could get some writing done. This was not a writing place.

I was hot, too hot. Maybe fresh water would help? I left the towel there and walked over to the spigot, filled a bowl with water and poured it over my head. Oh, that's better. Relief from the heat.

I refilled the bowl and poured it over my head again. Refreshing. This was better.

I returned to the slab and lay down, keeping the towel next to me in case someone walked in. I wondered if there were cameras in the room, recording; I was too hot to care.

I have low blood pressure, so saunas aren't a good idea for me. I poured a few bowls of water over my head and went into the next room.

A smaller room. Not hot, hallelujah.

I wrapped the thin Turkish towel around and around me and laid down on the marble slab. This experience would be improved with a nice mattress under me. This slab was cold; it reminded me of the time I went for surgery and they put me on a metal table in the operating room before they put me to sleep. That cold was uncomfortable. This cold marble was just right.

A man walked into my room. I didn't know this was a coed experience. No worries, I was wrapped up.

The man was about my age and the only thing he was wearing was a towel around his waist. He moved around the room. I figured he was going to lie on the other marble slab.

No. This was my worker.

A naked man wearing a towel was going to give me my treatments: a rubbing down, a soap massage and an oil massage?

My Turkish friends swear by these treatments. This wasn't about that term, FOMO or "Fear of Missing Out." I wanted the relaxation and spiritual renewal these treatments promised. I'd been having trouble sleeping on the road; I was tired all the time. Would a treatment help me rest?

My worker moved my writing bag out of the way and asked me to lie back on the slab, which surprised me; when did I sit up? He put on a white glove, kind of like an oven mitt made from coarse material, and began "buffing" my right arm. He made little circles with the glove, like he was polishing me, one inch at a time.

He worked quietly, head bent towards my arm. Polishing. Polishing. It fell somewhere between good and uncomfortable on the spectrum of skin care. I relaxed. This wasn't so bad. I watched him work, methodically.

He moved from my arm to my leg. Lower leg first, then upper leg. The reviews on the internet swore that this hamam was different because there were only male attendants, but that women should not worry; the men never cross a line or touch inappropriately.

I figured they wouldn't be in business for long if they did, right?

I've had massages by men before, but they do so much draping with sheets that I never felt exposed. My worker asked me something in Turkish. I had no idea what he was asking. He pointed to the towel. Oh, so he wants to move the towel, you know, drape it better.

Okay. We can do that.

He gently unwound the towel and had me lie down without it. Hello, towel? Then he twisted it into a diaper-like shape. My lower private area was covered, the rest of me was exposed.

Oh. So, really?

He continued polishing. My stomach. My upper chest. Methodically, carefully. I turned over and the diaper was repositioned—a hint of modesty. He polished my back, one inch at a time. I was pretty sure that my back had never had so much attention. He knew when to stop buffing one area to move to another before too much skin was removed. Every bit of my body was rubbed, except the area under the diaper and my breasts.

May I recommend a butt polish to anyone who's never had one?

It was strange to have a man work this intimately on my body. A man I didn't know. He showed no interest in me. He didn't try to talk or meet my eyes. His focus was on my skin.

For the past three weeks I'd traveled full time, walking for up to ten hours a day as I explored new places. My shoulders were sore from picking up my suitcase and putting it in a bin over my head, or wheeling it over cobblestones or carrying it up multiple flights of stairs.

I slept in a different bed every few nights and any routine I followed during normal life at home was not a part of my travel life. I had no complaints; the excitement of travel drives me, but my body was ready to work out some of the kinks.

He poured bowls of warm water over my body to wash away the dead skin, which explained why I couldn't have a mattress on the slab. More water, and more again.

He poured soap into a large bowl in the sink, then filled it with water. He put a piece of material that looked like a pillowcase into the water and "scooped" up bubbles. He held the material over me, and gently squeezed it; foam came out of the cloth and covered me.

I laughed. How did he get so many bubbles from simple soap? He could sell this formula. He dipped the cloth back into the bowl and scooped up more bubbles, then he squeezed them over my body.

You know how when you bathe a small child, you mold bubbles and place them on the kid's chin and give him or her a soap beard?

That's what I had, a soap beard, only it covered my whole body: a mountain of bubbles over my body. If anyone took my photo at this moment, it would show zero skin or limbs. I was a giant bubble mountain with a head sticking out one end.

He started massaging the bubbles into my arms and legs, then poured water over me and added more bubbles to do it again. This? This was relaxing.

All of the places that got buffed earlier were massaged with the foam. He spent extra time working on my feet. Could he tell they were sore?

He worked diligently, focusing on the soap and adding more bubbles when necessary. I was so relaxed that I might have fallen asleep here, on a marble slab in a random hamam in the south of Turkey.

The worker had me turn on my stomach, repositioned the diaper and placed a round pillow under my ankles which helped take the pressure off my knees. He covered the back of my body with soap until there was a mountain of soap, and then the back of my body got the same soapy foamy treatment.

If you had told me that a massage with soap would be relaxing, I would have doubted your ability to define comfort. This was an ancient tradition dating back to the Ottoman empire in the 1500s; I was an instant fan.

And though there was a practically naked man (!) working on me, there was nothing sexual about the touch or the movements, any more than going to the dentist is sexual or having a dermatologist scan your body looking for lumps. This procedure was work. Cleaning. Massaging. Skin care.

There was more to come, not bad for the price: a two-hour treatment for under $40 including the tip.

After the massage, he rinsed me with bowl after bowl of water; some bowls were room temperature, others were unexpectedly hot. The cold one shocked me. Then he wrapped me in three different towels, one for my body, one around my shoulders and one for my head. I followed him back to the reception area.

Wait, I'm going to sit here, naked under my towel, around people?

But then someone put a tray of fruit out for me and a cup of the famed apple tea. I forgot about my discomfort and started eating the perfectly ripe fruit. I felt a little dehydrated; the fruit was just what I needed.

I talked to the receptionist, a charming twenty-something. He was

Turkish and had worked here for a year and a half. He sat in a wheelchair and had the use of one hand; the rest of his body was paralyzed. As a special education teacher, I loved that this man was given a job. And where did he learn to speak English so well?

As I inhaled the fruit, he told me his story. Mid-twenties. Graduated college with a math degree two years ago. His uncle owned the place. He routinely traveled with his family to different countries, for the fun of travel.

I asked what nationality came to the hamam most often and he said Russian, followed by European.

He told me that his family leaves his wheelchair at the desk after his shift, and they carry him to the car, which is a great way to get around the many staircases.

I told him that I was a special education teacher and that he was #2 for being the best English speaker I'd met in Turkey so far.

"Who was number one?" he asked, and we talked about English acquisition skills and became Facebook friends; he wanted to read about my adventures in Turkey.

When it was time for my oil massage, my same worker came to get me. He was wearing clothes. Clothes! I was led to a different room for a typical half-hour oil massage.

I'd been exfoliated, cleaned and now was getting an intense oil massage. I'd read online that people get addicted to these treatments; I could see why.

At the end of my session, he suggested I lie on the table and sleep for a while.

So I did.

DAY 22: ÇIRALI: TAXI

I came upon the accident after it happened and watched as the driver stared at a hole his minivan gashed into a parked car. These streets are narrow, why was he backing his car around a parked car? People walked by, rubbernecking, and the driver yelled at them in rapid Turkish which probably translated to something like, "Mind your own business."

I'd only been in Antalya for three days but after many hours of walking the streets, I was surprised that there weren't multiple car accidents every day. The narrow streets would be enough of a challenge, but cars park along these streets, and the only way to get past is to drive around those parked cars and hope you don't hit a wall.

I wandered wherever my feet wanted to go, glad that I'd finally figured out the layout of the town; it was easier than I first thought. I walked to the harbor then found my way to the series of parks lining the sea. The view was superb at 7:00 AM.

I passed through Hadrian's Gate, on my way back to an ATM that claimed my bank wouldn't charge a fee for using it, which is a wonder of the traveling world, no ATM fees? As I wandered away from the tourist area, I felt more at home and reminded myself that I don't like sleeping in the tourist areas, preferring diversity in the things I see and do. What was I thinking when I booked Kaleiçi?

My favorite ice cream shop, hidden on a side street far from the tourist corner, wasn't open yet. Too bad. I'd like a before-breakfast ice cream. People shared the sidewalk with me as they headed to work. Many women wore heels.

I spotted an evil-eye symbol imbedded in a building and realized I'd moved from discovering them as if I were on a scavenger hunt, to looking at them and feeling protected. How did that change come about?

Maybe it had to do with seeing literally thousands of these symbols in sidewalks, as art hanging on walls, woven into carpets, as decorations in jewelry, and as souvenir trinkets.

There were other subtle changes in me in my three weeks of traveling through Turkey. I no longer wanted to photograph every woman wearing a head scarf. When people spoke to me in Turkish, I was better at guessing the topic or the idea or the intention and didn't feel the need to give the "I don't understand" pantomime.

The store vendors got used to me passing by their shops without buying anything; most of them gave up on getting a big sale out of me. All except for this one carpet store worker who greeted me as I walked by. As far as I could tell, the man works every day from 6:30 AM and is still working at dusk when I head inside.

"How the town today?" he asked me in English.

"Slow," I said. "It's early."

He nodded. "I think today you buy at carpet."

I smiled at his continued ability to turn every conversation towards buying a carpet. "No, thank you."

"We mail it you house. It be on floor when you go home and remember good Turkey. This essential for future remembering."

It would be cool if the UPS driver opened my packages and displayed the contents around my house. Maybe he could dust while he's there or fix the shed door that needs tending. "I am a teacher," I tell the vendor. "I only have enough money to look, never to buy."

He continues, "Teachers best customers." He steps closer.

"Teachers good taste. Most our customers teachers." He points to me. "Teachers understand quality. Our carpet they like."

He'd be better off saying that teachers deserve a magic carpet after long hours in small classrooms, surrounded by children who would rather play video games. I'd buy a magic carpet.

After breakfast I checked out of my hotel and asked the owner to call a taxi for me. He remembered where I was going from past conversations, and said that he was building apartments in Çirali and wished me a very good vacation.

I wondered how many lira this ride to the bus station would cost.

The taxi driver put my suitcase in the trunk; I worried that we would drive around in circles as he tried to find his way out of the confusing one-way streets of Kaleiçi.

When I was safely in the car, he started the car and put the air conditioning on right away, which doesn't always happen. That's a win right there.

Then he hit reverse.

Wait. He was driving backwards?

He drove backwards down the street. These narrow streets. Past parked cars. Around corners. He stopped and repositioned the car, then continued driving backwards. Around another turn. Down another street. There were no seatbelts. Or helmets.

I didn't know whether to look behind me where we were going, or look out the front window to where we'd been, or close my eyes. I did a little of each. I wanted to tell him I'd be willing to pay extra money, if necessary, to drive forward around the block, but had trouble forming words.

Finally we got out of the old quarter and he turned the car around and drove forward. My breathing slowed and I watched the city from the comfort of the car. Breathe. Breathe.

The driver offered to drive me to Çirali for 50 euros. Note to self, it's never a good idea to stay in places that charge in a currency that's foreign to where I'm traveling and where I live. When I declined, he picked up the radio and told his dispatch that I didn't want a taxi ride to Çirali.

I really think that's what he said. And it made me feel like there was a network of people trying to manipulate me, like the movie, *The Truman Show*. If there is such a network of such people, please tell them I'd like the spicy tomato paste and the cream with honey added back on my breakfast buffets because I'm missing them so.

At the bus station I bought my ticket and went outside. I easily located a man managing the area and said, "Çirali?" He pointed to a bus, and a young man in street clothes took my suitcase from me and checked my ticket.

I'd learned from my time here that managers stand around bus stations directing people; that's why they don't have signs: they use people. And every bus has up to three staff: one to drive, one to deal with the luggage and one to serve complimentary drinks.

It was dubbed a 90-minute bus ride, but that timing didn't start until we'd spent an hour driving around the city picking people up. It wasn't an issue for me, I had time.

The bus stopped and some people got off at a restaurant in the middle of nowhere. I got off and asked the driver as I pointed to the ground, "Çirali?"

He nodded, but had a worried look on his face, which put a worried look on my face.

I knew I had to transfer to another bus. A group of people walked across the parking lot and climbed into a minibus parked in the shade. I figured this was my bus, too.

I put my suitcase in the back, then showed the driver my address. He shook his head, so I started fumbling with my phone, looking for a map of where I was going, when the driver had a woman speak to me.

"This is not the bus to Çirali," she said in perfect English.

I laughed; glad I didn't get on that bus. I said to the driver, "Çirali?"

He pointed to a chair, then motioned holding a phone to his ear to let me know that he'd call somebody at the bus company.

I thanked him. Before he drove away, he locked eyes with the manager of this oasis and pointed to me.

The manager walked to me and said, "Çirali." And after an hour wait, put me on the right bus.

It was only a 15-minute ride to my next home for a few days, a cabin community in an orange grove on the Mediterranean Sea. My cabin was a family-sized unit. The man in charge had made good on my reservation when the dates got boggled in his system, but he had to put me in a larger unit. I'd have to pay for the extra space.

I didn't care. It was time to slow down; having more room to spread out was a gift.

I was happy to be so close to the beach and so close to town.

In Çirali visiting the ancient city of Olympos.

Holly Winter Huppert's new Turkish towel and 100% cotton shirt.

DAY 23: ÇIRALI: OLYMPOS

My guidebook stated that the ruins of Olympos were only three kilometers from town, I was willing to walk it. Just to be sure, I asked the manager of the bungalow community where I'm staying to explain how to get there.

He repeated the 3-kilometer distance.

Perfect! I started my walk at 4:30, when the temperature had dropped to 95 degrees. I walked into town and stopped at a café for a mini orange soda in a glass bottle. Çirali was a small town without any high-rise buildings or major industry. Turtles nested on the beaches at night, so this area was protected. Only small businesses can be a part of this community. A small, friendly, dusty beach-town was just what I was looking for.

I sipped my soda, so delicious, and stared out at the Mediterranean Sea, procrastinating my mission. After a while I continued my walk but was distracted by a café in the shade right on the beach. I stopped for a tea and admired the ocean views.

So in truth I don't know how long it took me to walk to Olympos, and it doesn't really matter because I love to walk. But I noticed that after I walked at least three kilometers, I saw a sign that showed the distance to Olympos to be three more kilometers.

Seriously?

I might have taken a taxi, but decided to walk as much as I could while traveling so I could save money for more exciting things than air conditioning on a hot day. But I also like to walk because it's the only way for me to truly explore an area.

It's true, first I complain about the lack of signage, then complain when there are signs. Was it possible that three kilometers was a code word for—2-hour walk?

I arrived at Olympos around 7:00 PM, which was later than I thought I'd get there, but the advantage was that the site closes at that exact time; I got in for free. I thought I'd poke around for a few minutes, be sure I knew my way, then return tomorrow.

But when I got inside, there was so much to see. A murky green pond reflecting an ancient structure. Old crumbling buildings that I wanted to investigate. Right. Now. There were little bridges to walk over and hills to climb for better vistas.

I wasn't the only one taking advantage of the free entrance. Hundreds of people walked along the path. Many of them were staying in the town of Olympos, on the far side of the archaeological site. I walked to the town and wanted to try the melon ice cream that was known in this area.

And though I pointed to a sign in front of the dessert shop that said "Melon Ice Cream" in two languages, they couldn't figure out what I was talking about. Finally they picked a flavor for me, lemon, which was a good second choice.

I walked back along the beach that all information written about the area claimed was a sandy beach. It was a sandy beach—if you dug under layers and layers of small rocks, you'd find sand.

If you walk along the rocky water's edge without shoes, you will move at a pace so slow the other beachgoers will laugh at you. (Okay. I'm raising my hand on this one.) Walking on a sandy beach with bare feet and walking on a rocky beach with bare feet are not the same thing.

I walked part of the way home along the rockiest part of the beach because I was wearing my sandals. It was hard work, which was good for me, I'm always looking for a good workout when I'm traveling. But

I became so out of breath and so overheated that I thought it would be best to get back to the road for the rest of the walk home.

There was a produce stand and grapes seemed like a good idea. I stepped inside and stood in front of the fan, cooling off. The woman running the place laughed at me and might have said something like "It's cooler in the shade, remember that!"

The owners of the family-run restaurants along the dirt road that runs through town hose it down several times a day to keep the dust to a minimum. Many people walk along the road that separates the many hotels and bungalow colonies from the beach.

I passed a sign that said my exact bungalow colony was one kilometer away. I've learned a lot in my twenty-three days in Turkey, and decided that the sign was likely underestimating the distance.

I stopped in a restaurant for my daily lamb shish with asparagus and homemade yogurt, and then when I was done, I tackled the 40-minute walk back to my home for the night.

DAY 24: ÇIRALI: PASSPORT

I needed to move my passport from my purse to my suitcase; I didn't need to carry it while I walked around. If someone were to stop me and ask for it, I had a photocopy I could show.

I went to move my passport out of my purse, but it wasn't in my purse. Hmm. It must be in the mesh zippered pocket in my suitcase, the other place I keep it. I pushed a few things out of the way and checked the pocket. It wasn't there.

Hmm. These are the only two places I put my passport. I never lay it around.

When you travel outside the US, each country has rules for how you carry your ID. In Vietnam, I was instructed to only carry a photocopy. In Cuba I was told I'd better hide my passport incredibly well, because thieves would try to steal it, so I only carried a copy. Here in Turkey I was told to always carry the passport itself, but really...even on the beach? I should carry the original document to the hamam?

Today was going to be a combination beach day and exploring more ancient ruins, so I wanted to leave it in the bungalow.

I searched the hiding places again. Not there. I took everything out of my purse. Not there. I took everything out of my day bag. Not there.

In Turkey, checkpoints are set up along roads. Once when I was with the archaeologist we drove up to a "pop up" checkpoint.

He said to me, "Take you paper out."

Oops. I figured I didn't need it to walk around Ephesus.

"You don't have it?" he asked, after I explained that I had a copy on me.

We drove up to the checkpoint and he told the police officer that he was an archaeologist going to Ephesus, and we were waved through. After that I carried my passport everywhere I went in Selçuk.

I had the passport when I checked into the bungalow community. It had to be around here. I went through my purse and my day bag, again. Slower this time, organizing as I took everything out and clearing away old receipts and trash. Everything in my purse and day bag was lying on the counter in the kitchen. There was no question: my passport wasn't there.

I checked the dining area and the bedroom. No passport anywhere.

When I was on the bus from Isparta to Antalya, the bus got pulled over at a checkpoint and several unsmiling officials climbed onto the bus. The lead made an announcement in Turkish. Everyone on the bus was very quiet.

I waited. Nope. No English translation.

The men across from me took out their wallets and handed the man their ID cards. I didn't know if they wanted identification from all of us, or a few select people.

I handed the man my passport.

He held it a few inches from his face and studied the cover, sure he'd found a fake. Then opened it to the page with my photo, which was taken at Walgreens when they had a sale. It wasn't a good photo of me, but it only cost $5. Sitting here with an official who would decide my fate with a photo that doesn't look like me made me realize that cheap passport photos are a terrible idea.

Note taken.

He flipped through the pages of the passport, looking to see where I'd been. I wondered if he would link the places I've been into some kind of...plot. He found the page with the stamp showing I entered the country through Istanbul and held his gaze there for several moments, then snapped it shut and added it to the stack of documents in his hands. He kept my passport. He walked through the bus collecting every ID from every person on the bus, then took the documents off the bus and into a nearby building.

The driver and his staff got off the bus, too. It was as if they didn't care about our fates; their lack of interest in our futures made me feel a little lonely and a lot vulnerable. The bus staff sat drinking tea and smoking cigarettes at a little area with tables, and I wondered how long it would take to check the identification of so many people on a large bus with every seat taken.

Ask any Turkish person, and he or she will tell you that these controls are good and that they make the country safer. I'm not sure if they are looking for terrorists or illegal aliens or bank robbers, but sitting on the very quiet bus waiting for them to process our identifications, my mind wandered towards fear.

I practiced saying the words, "I want to talk to someone in the American Consulate," which was going to make people who don't speak English shrug their shoulders. That sentence loses its punch when you can't understand it.

After twenty minutes or so the official returned the pile of IDs to the driver and we were free to go. The worker who served drinks took the pile from the driver and returned our identifications to us. The advantage of being the only American on the bus was that it was easy to get my ID back. I returned it to the front zippered pocket of my purse.

Okay.

It was almost time to panic. Seriously, my passport had to be here. I rechecked both places, twice. I checked a few more places where I might have put it. Nope. Nothing.

I walked to the manager's office; he had to have it. When hotel staff in Turkey process a new guest, they must make a photocopy of the ID and send it to the police department. Maybe my passport was sitting in the photocopier, waiting for me. The manager wasn't in his office.

Hmm. I sent him an email asking if he had my passport, then left for a morning of exploring.

I walked all the way back to the ruins of Olympos and drank a whole bottle of water along the way. I bought two more bottles at the entrance, paid my entry fee, and entered an ancient city.

There's something about ancient ruins that excites me. It's proof of history that wasn't readily available in upstate New York; other than finding the occasional arrowheads from the Native Americans of long ago, we don't have things or buildings that are very old.

Where I live now, in Kingston, New York, there is a church called the "Old Dutch Church" that was originally built in 1660, which makes it over three hundred years old. The church is used for many different community functions and is still used as a church. It's the pride of Kingston and the seat of many historical reenactments. Schoolchildren visit the church, because it's so...old. Three hundred and fifty-nine years old is something to celebrate where I live.

So you can see why being around ruins that are thousands of years old is so exciting to me.

I figured I'd be in the ruins for an hour or two and then make my way back to my hotel to deal with the passport. But five hours later, I was still wandering through the site, wide eyed. I wanted to touch every wall and walk through every door. I climbed the mountain to get closer to the ruins on top. There were thorn bushes around the top ruin, and they drew blood from my arms and legs as I passed them, but I barely noticed. Those people of long ago could look one way and see the Mediterranean Sea, then turn the other way and see a dense forest, well, if it were a forest thousands of years ago. Best views ever.

I sat to hydrate and realized I needed to reapply sunscreen but didn't have any more with me. Either I had to sit in the shade for the next four hours or find sunscreen. I saw a woman applying sunscreen on her face and walked up to her and asked if I could have some.

"Sure," she said. It felt like a miracle that I found someone who spoke English, albeit with a British accent.

We sat in the shade for a while comparing stories: I teach special education; she is a teacher's assistant with a 14-year-old son who needs extra support. He was back in the room sleeping because the sensory load of being in a new place exhausted him.

She showed me a red lump on her arm. Spider bite? The towns around here are so small, she couldn't buy an antihistamine and it was concerning as the lump was growing.

I had extra Benadryl in my room and offered her some. I entered my name into her phone as "Holly has Benadryl" and without discussing it, she entered her name into my phone, "Lorraine Bite." She and her friend and their children would meet up with me later to pick up the medicine.

With my new sunscreen protecting me, I spent a few more hours exploring. I was low on water. And overheated. And tired. I bought more water at the exit and started the very long, very hot walk back home.

I stopped in the manager's office. He said, "Did you find your passport?"

"No," I said. "Do you have it?"

He opened drawers and dug under piles. "I don't have it," he said. "You have to find it."

I walked slowly back to my room. I was sweating so much it looked like I had showered with my clothes on. Rather than searching for the passport right away, I drank a bottle of water, then another. I showered, washed my clothes in the bathroom sink and hung them on the clothesline on my porch. I sat under the air conditioner, wishing it would work, then ate a snack.

Refreshed, I resumed the search. When I removed everything from my suitcase, I found the passport right away, in the "dirty clothes" pocket. There? How did it get there?

That's the thing about traveling alone; you can't blame others when you do something unexplainable. Was I that tired when I checked in?

I sent a message to the manager who replied with a stern, "Don't lose it again." I wanted to respond with a "Thanks, Dad," because he's twenty years younger than I am, but didn't think that kind of jest would cross cultural lines.

I wondered if he would have turned me in if I didn't find my ID?

My new British friends came for a visit and we hung out on the beach while Lorraine popped a few Benadryls. Her friend and her friend's son went for a swim. It was the best time of day on the beach, nearly sundown.

Her friend's son wanted to pick a prickly pear off a cactus as this is the time of year they are ripe. His mother gave him stern directions: you cannot use your hands. You cannot use your clothes. It was one of those logic puzzles I used to give to my middle school students where there isn't a good answer.

Her son was not deterred.

Both boys ran off and I compared travel stories with my new friends as we watched the swelling go down on Lorraine's arm. Her friend had been to Turkey several times and had the most beautiful Turkish towel, a cloth that's multicolored, woven with tassels on the ends.

Note to self: Buy a Turkish towel.

When the boys returned, the friend's son had a prickly pear cactus stuck on a stick, a brilliant plan. His mother carefully took it off and we each took turns tasting the inside flesh. Sweet, like a pear and filled with hard, slippery seeds that were also edible.

There's something about sitting on a beach with strangers who have become new friends, pulling prickly spears from my fingers as I watched the sun set on the Turquoise Coast of Turkey. My thoughts didn't lean towards what I am missing at home or the inconveniences of the day.

I watched as the sky slowly turned pink, dug my feet into the sand and tried to suck the prickly pear spears from my fingers.

~

Photo next page: The ancient city of Olympus

DAY 25: ÇIRALI: BOY

A two-year-old boy chased a stray cat until he saw me sitting at a nearby table in a restaurant. He approached my table and started speaking to me in Turkish. I nodded my head for a while, agreeing with everything he said, but he made a point about something that he felt was important and tilted his head to the side, waiting for me to respond.

"Hello sweet boy," I said. "Does your mommy or your daddy tell you what cute curls you have?"

The boy stared at me and his mouth opened.

"It's okay if you don't understand my words," I said, softly. "Maybe you can understand even if you don't know my words."

I smiled across the restaurant at his mother and gave her a little wave, to let her know he wasn't bothering me.

He looked at his mother and yelled something to her. She stood and walked over, but slowly as if she wanted her son to have the space to figure it out for himself.

"I noticed you like cats," I said. "Do you have a cat at home?"

His mother joined us, and I said to her, "He is beautiful, and those curls." I made a curling motion with my hand.

She smiled.

He talked to her in a very serious tone, then looked at me.

She smiled, nodded her head and said something softly in Turkish.

The boy approached me and gave me a fast, hard hug.

I smiled. "Hey, thanks for the hug."

The boy stood there, pulling on my shirt but I couldn't tell why.

The mother said, "He want kiss you."

I smiled. I put my cheek down and he gave me a peck.

I smiled at the boy and wanted to tell his mother what a sweet kid he is; perhaps she could tell what I was thinking.

The boy walked away, then turned back and blew me a kiss.

I laughed, "Oh, really?" and returned the gesture and he laughed. We blew kisses to each other for a few rounds, and then he saw the stray cat sitting nearby and I was forgotten.

As it should be.

My evening plans weren't until later, so I headed out to the beach.

A large family was building a sandcastle where the kids directed the adults in rapid Turkish. A three-year-old boy and a five-year-old girl issued commands: Towers higher. Moat needs more water. A window here. More water in the moat. The various adults scrambled to do the kids' bidding. A worker made a wrong move and knocked down a wall, the kids squealed in protest. He quickly rebuilt the wall and the kids were right there to tell him how to do it.

Along the shoreline, other children were bouncing on brightly colored tubes in the water. I could hear them laughing from where I sat. One fell off her tube and went under the water. She came up crying, then climbed back on the tube to continue to play.

I love watching children play: laughing, experimenting, failing, trying again, succeeding.

A grandfather, a father and a son who might have been five years old found a place on the sand to fly kites: three generations of kite fliers. The father got the kite in the air and his son ran under the magic that lifted the kite into the sky. Then the boy ran to take over the holding of the strings; within seconds, the kite fell to the ground. The little boy ran to fetch it, and the whole scenario began again.

As it should be.

It was time to meet my British friends for an after-dinner hike. They secured a guide who was more than happy to let me join the group for a nighttime visit to the Chimera, a place up in the mountains where natural fire burns out of a rocky outcropping twenty-four hours a day.

Why is there a fire burning in the middle of nowhere? There are two bodies of thought: It's either a fire-breathing monster that was killed as part of an ancient story, as in he's not dead yet, or the flames are part of a natural gas leak.

I personally subscribe to the idea that the fire has to do with a monster but wanted to go and see it for myself. Visitors brew tea over the flames and cook breakfast. We were going to roast some late-night marshmallows. I bought chocolate to go with our dessert feast.

I walked twenty-five minutes and made it to the meeting place by 9:00 PM and texted my friends that I was there. They were driving from the opposite direction with a driver who was happy to pick me up on the way.

The driver had them text back, saying he wanted me to meet them somewhere else. I texted my friends to remind him that I was walking, and it would be better for all of us if he drove to get me.

He refused.

But... I told them where I was, again, at the designated meeting spot. The driver had them text back that he didn't want to drive that way. He would drive me home later, but I needed to walk to meet them now.

On and on we texted. I couldn't jump in a taxi from where I waited, and if I walked to meet them, it was another twenty-five-minute walk —without streetlights.

The driver sent me a directive: be there in fifteen minutes or miss the hike.

Yeah? No.

Sadly, I texted them to go without me.

Sad. I dragged my feet all the way home. I really wanted to go.

I got back to the bungalow. I really wanted to go. Sometimes a do-over isn't possible. I would leave Çirali tomorrow morning, which meant that I'd never stare the fire monster in the eye.

I don't always get my way. I sat outside my bungalow and listened to the 24-hour Rooster Radio and ate some chocolate.

No fire monster tonight, but other adventures await.

The windshield is close enough to touch when sitting on the steps of the bus.

The harbor of Kaş, Turkey.

DAY 26: KAŞ: BUS

I was the only one from the first bus that was heading south for the second leg of the trip. Everyone else was heading back to Antalya. A woman on the minibus told me to be very careful crossing the highway, the traffic moves fast.

She was right. I paused at the side of the road and watched the cars speeding by. This was a major highway, how was I going to get across?

You don't realize how wide a four-lane highway is until you're standing at the edge, where the only breeze is the cars and buses and tractor-trailers whizzing by on a hundred-degree cloudless day. There was a small break in traffic, so I ran as fast as I could, pulling my suitcase behind me, to the median in the center where I gasped for breath. It might be easier to run across the highway if I weren't holding my breath.

I had to wait several long minutes to finish my sprint and finally stood on that far side of the highway, wondering if I was sure how to flag down my bus.

There was no shade; I put on my hat. I'm the only one I've seen in the entire country of Turkey who wears a hat away from the beach.

A bus approached and I made the downward motion with my hand as they do in the Middle East. Could this be my bus? I'd only been standing there for twenty minutes, but I was ready for air conditioning and some forward motion. There was no plan "B" if my bus didn't appear. Plan "A" was to stand there until my bus came.

The bus stopped right in front of me and the sign in the window read "Kaş." Relief. This was the bus I was waiting for.

I waited for the attendant to store my suitcase under the bus and smiled my biggest smile as I climbed on.

The driver said something, and I reached for money to pay. He shook his head and said something. I said, "Kaş." He nodded and pointed to the steps I was standing on.

Was he motioning for me to leave? How do you beg in Turkish?

Someone stepped forward and said that I must sit on the seat on the stairs as the bus was full.

I wanted to argue because there were plenty of empty seats. I could see empty seats.

The driver pointed again, told me in Turkish to sit on the jump seat. As a former flight attendant, I've seen my share of jump seats, but never knew buses had them. There is one right over the stairs. My left foot sat on the step at normal level, my right foot dangled in midair and couldn't reach the lower step.

We stopped at a rest stop and many people got off the bus. The driver told me to wait five minutes, as the attendant translated. Sorry, but I wasn't waiting. I wanted a seat with air conditioning. I found an empty window seat in the back and settled in. The driver came on the bus and pegged me and another woman to come back to the front. I got the jump seat again, and the woman had to sit on the aisle floor in the center. No seat belts for either of us. Or air conditioning. Or comfort.

The driver chatted with us as he drove. He also did some paperwork, made phone calls and smoked a few cigarettes. He always drove at least twenty kilometers over the limit, even going around those gruesome turns. He wasn't afraid to swerve into the oncoming traffic lane to help us get around a slow car.

You see a lot when you're sitting within arm's reach of the windshield.

In Turkey, bus drivers don't just drive or collect money or answer questions about "How much longer?" They consider the bus to be an enormous puzzle. Many women can't sit next to men due to Muslim rules, so first the driver figures out how to keep the families together, and then he sits the couples together. Finally he pairs the same-gender passengers together. Many drivers ignore the seat numbers on the bus tickets.

A man offered me a seat next to him and I said yes, but the driver wasn't going to let me be disrespected in that way. I couldn't imagine what would happen if there were someone who had switched genders or was gender neutral.

Nobody complained when he made them move, and nobody asked to remain where they were. He was the captain of our traveling souls.

It's one of the big differences between our countries, that the men were given the VIP seats and the women were pressed against the front window. I think in the United States, men would have been given the uncomfortable seats.

Luckily, we only had to sit there for an hour or so, then some men in the back got off. The driver insisted that this woman and I still sit together even though there were many, many empty seats.

Okay. Fine.

I was going to Kaş, another town on the Mediterranean Sea and part of the Turquoise Coast of Turkey. I had a four-minute walk from where the bus let me off to my hotel; that proximity was not luck, it took hours of planning. I would only stay in this hotel for one night, then move to another hotel for the next few nights.

I left my stuff in the smallest hotel room I've ever seen, which means it's even smaller than that room I had in Italy where I had to leave my suitcase in the hall.

I kept the suitcase in this room, but only because I had a twin bed this time. I could reach my hands out and touch both walls at the same time.

I tried out the bed for a "Welcome to a new town rest," and wasn't impressed with the lumps in the mattress. It was a cheap lumpy bed, the price I paid for getting the last room in the city for the night at $10. I didn't mind, I'd curl up on the floor in a corner if it meant I could travel to a new place.

I wanted meze for dinner and found the perfect restaurant. For under $8, I got a sampling of eight different appetizers, or meze. (It would have been ten samplings, but two of them had gluten.) The dish was meant to be shared among a large group of people. I ate it all, everything from spicy beans to garlic yogurt to roasted eggplant to carrot salad. I wanted to eat this way every day.

I wandered the town, up the hill, down to the dock, around the outside edges. There's so much to see here in Kaş ; it's a perfect combination of tourists and locals. I bought a prickly pear cactus from a street vendor. He cut the fruit open and slid the fruit out of the shell into my hand. It dripped through my fingers and I helped myself to some napkins. It was perfectly ripe and since he carved it out of the rind, I got no prickles in my hands while eating it.

Such an improvement.

On the Island of Meis in Greece, Holly Winter Huppert ate a lunch that included a baby octopus.

The small opening under the rock leads to the Blue Cave.

DAY 27: GREECE: BLUE CAVE

G reece was only a 20-minute ferry ride away from Kaş. Though it felt like I was cheating on my love of Turkey, I decided a day trip was prudent.

I found a tourist agency due to spectacular signage and stepped inside to ask where the ferry office was. The agency sold the tickets for the ferry and they had air conditioning—perfect.

The man behind the counter was filled with information on the island trip, when to go to the Blue Cave, where to eat lunch and what to watch out for on the island. I was open to suggestions because I had never heard of the Greek island of Meis. He also fixed my WhatsApp, which had refused to work from the moment I entered Turkey. Others had tried to get it working but couldn't. He hit a few buttons and it worked.

I am easily impressed by the genius of strangers.

Since I was leaving the country, I had to deal with passport control. Either I could leave my passport with the agency overnight or I could arrive an hour early; I opted for the early arrival.

When I arrived on the day of the journey, I watched the workings of the agency from a comfortable chair under the map of Turkey. There were many group trips going out for the day, fishing, sightseeing and swimming on distant beaches. The tickets for these events were spread out on the owner's desk. Once he got the name of the person who paid, he'd hand over the tickets for that person's group.

Then there was another class of excursions where the owner kept the printed information in his front right pants pocket. I watched as the two different groups came into the office and the owner reached into his pocket and found the right paper, then folded the other back into his pocket.

The first family, six people, had children from about 10 to 17 years old. They sat across from me on more comfortable chairs and figured out the logistics with the owner, whom they had met the day before when they booked the trip.

In a quiet moment, I asked how much they paid for the full-day private boat tour and the dad said that he paid 800 lira, which included the entire day and two hot meals. And the owner of their private boat would fly a drone to record their fun. While he told me about the perks, I did some mental math: That's just under $150 for six people for the whole day?

I was paying $45 for my ferry ticket. He got a great deal. The dad agreed with me, shrugged, and the family followed the owner out of the agency to be delivered to their private boat excursion.

After a while, a family of four walked in with two children under the age of ten and the owner took the other piece of paper from his pocket. I chatted with the new family about Kaş and where they were from, and got around to asking how much they paid for their excursion.

Eight hundred euros. Including lunch.

I hid my shock, nodded my head and asked how he got such a good deal. He told me he found it online. The owner gave me a low sign with his hand mimicking a "no" fashion, to be sure I didn't compare the two purchases with the man.

So one family paid $150 for the day and another paid $972 for the day? Sure, they had different boats and different itineraries. I hope the second family got a day that was over six times better than the first family was getting.

I don't know the moral of this story. Shopper beware, or research when you show up, or pay whatever you want?

Chatting with me when we were alone, the owner told me his job was the best because most of the hard work was done by 10:00 AM. He offered me a position at his travel agency, if I wanted to move to Kaş. I smiled and accepted the offer, if ever...

An hour after I handed in my passport, the agency sent me to the ferry's main office to wait some more. Their office was a storefront near the marina, not a part of the marina; no wonder I couldn't find it.

When it was fifteen minutes past when the boat was supposed to depart, a worker gathered a bunch of us travelers from all over the world and walked us to the ferry where we waited together in a giant mass. A passport control officer appeared carrying a large box of passports. One at a time he called out a name, that person would step forward and the officer would compare the photo ID to the person.

He held my photo next to my face for an extra beat or two. I know, I know: better photo next time.

The trip over was majestic. The white houses of Turkey gleamed in the sun against the bluest water, like a child's simple drawing without shadows or muted colors. The water reminded me of a young girl wearing eye shadow for the first time where you want to whisper "too much" so she might tone it down to a more natural level. If you were to show the color of this water to this same young girl, she might respond by noting that clearly you've never been to the Mediterranean's Turquoise Coast; light turquoise is a natural color.

Greece beckoned, a lone flag on a rock, and the best part of all was that I didn't feel seasick.

For years people have told me I won't feel seasick if I do this or that or buy this or that. Trust me when I tell you, nothing works. But today was a calm day and my stomach remained flipless.

After passing through passport control, I was free to roam the town. Multilevel colorful mansions etched into the mountainside. The main street ran around the edges of the cove, with stores and restaurants spilling out onto the sidewalk and then reflecting in the water. It was all at once beautiful and peaceful and inviting.

The restaurant, Alexandra, that the man in the agency had

recommended, was around the cove, far from the docks. In front of the restaurant, the owner wore a clean white apron while he butchered a hunk of fresh tuna; he pushed his weight onto the knife to crack through the bones.

I wanted fresh seafood; I hit the jackpot.

It wasn't clear if the owner cut up fish on this special table to snag tourists like me who wanted fresh fish, or because it was easier to hose off the outside table after he finished.

I was the first customer of the day so I chose the best table, the one at the very edge of the sidewalk with a view of the hill; if I leaned too far left, I would fall into the water. I ordered the Greek salad, because when in Rome...and decided to try the octopus.

The salad arrived and that first bite of fresh feta cheese made my eyes water. Creamy. Salty. Briney. Just right. The tomatoes and cucumbers paired perfectly with the olives and the cheese; I didn't miss the lettuce or other cheeses served in my favorite Greek salads in the States.

When I ordered octopus in the past, I'd gotten a lump of cut-up pieces. Not today: I got a whole baby octopus on my plate: complete with round body and dangling legs. His eight legs were charred as if he'd swum over a fire pit. I felt guilty for ordering his death, so to speak, and vowed to eat every bite.

It was more meaty tasting than fishy and easy to cut. Once I got past the barbaric notion that I was eating something that was alive just hours ago, it was delicious, even craveable.

I sat in the shade taking in the view. The beauty of the water, the colors of the houses, the gleaming wares of the shops and the looming mountain behind it all filled me in a way a salad never could.

I sat in awe. This. Beauty. Now. It felt like I were the lone tourist visiting my own island, because the other tourists had stopped for lunch at restaurants closer to the docks. I sat alone, in peace, eating slowly while drinking in my surroundings.

Normally I eat fast, especially when there is exploring to do. There was a mountain to climb with an old castle on top. I was looking forward to walking behind the main street to see what was there; how did the locals live? And I wanted to check out the Blue Cave excursion that was first stop on most people's list for visiting the island.

But sitting there at that table, none of that mattered. If there's such a thing as an open-eyed-eating meditation, I was doing it. The staff left me alone as if they'd seen this kind of brain clearing before.

I sat for hours, absorbing. Time stopped, though a small part of me worried my ferry would leave and the day would end, and I would still be sitting at the closed restaurant staring into the darkness; I kept an eye on the time.

When the food was gone and I thought I might have overstayed my welcome, my waiter delivered three slices of vine-ripened watermelon. In Europe they never rush you through a meal; the longer you stay, the greater the compliment.

I sat and ate with the smallest bites possible as I permitted the feelings of peace to grow.

A man sitting behind me tapped me on the shoulder to get my attention and pointed to the water. I hadn't noticed that other customers were sitting outside with me; every table was taken.

There was a giant sea turtle swimming right next to me, begging for food. I grabbed my camera and took a few photos and talked to the man and his 14-year-old son, who were from Holland, while I finished my watermelon.

They invited me to join them on their Blue Cave tour and I thanked them for the invitation. I paid my bill with my credit card, then realized I only had two euros in cash to leave a tip because most of my money was in lira, darn it. Sorry, sweet waiter. Thanks for taking care of me. I hope you don't mind getting paid in lira.

The marina was filled with small boats with shade coverings which would have been the perfect touring boat to get to the cave, but the father, the son and I were the only guests on a motorboat without any covering or handles to hold on.

The owner of the agency had warned me that his wife's friend has permanent back problems from that boat ride, and that if they are going too fast it will be too bumpy and I must demand that they slow down.

A few minutes into the boat trip, I understood that message as the boat bounced and bounced in these constantly jarring movements. Permanent back damage? I had to try my darnedest to relax as the boat jammed its way along the ocean. Anyone who thinks that water provides a soft landing is wrong.

After one bump that had all of us scrambling to stay inside the boat, I gave the driver, Mr. Kosta, that same warning look we women have perfected over time: he would be struck by lightning or the plague or something equally tragic if he didn't slow down this very minute. And even though I had never met the captain before or said any words in Greek that he would understand, that look led to an immediate understanding: he slowed, and the bumps went away.

We got to a nondescript place next to a wall of rock and Mr. Kosta said, "Miss. You can swim?"

Was he throwing me out of the boat? "Yes," I said.

He asked, "You swim good?"

Why wasn't he asking the men if they could swim? "Yes. I swim very good."

He said, "You go now. You swim."

The father and I looked at each other. What were the chances that this was my last swim? I lived in Europe when I was younger and know that European men don't like to be corrected. Was I being punished for making him slow the boat?

"Just me?" I asked.

Mr. Kosta threw me an impatient wave. "You first."

The dad and I looked at each other. Was he sorry for inviting me to my death?

There was a place in the wall of rock behind the boat that was raised a bit. Was that slit the cave?

"You swim now, Miss."

From what I read about the Blue Cave, seals lived inside. I thought the boat was going to ride us into the cave so we could have a look around from the comfort and safety of the floating womb. Were seals territorial? Probably. If attacked, could I kick a seal in the knee? Do seals have knees?

He said louder, "You go swim now."

I turned my head so the men could change into their swimsuits; they thought we were staying in the boat too.

I took off my jewelry and put it into my bag while the captain continued to beg me to start swimming. What's the rush? I took off my shirt because my bathing suit top was under it. I would swim in my fast-drying shorts.

I sat on the edge of the boat. Afraid.

"Please, Miss," he said again. "Please swim now."

I told the father I was afraid to jump in; the son jumped in first. Yes, the children will lead us.

From sitting on the edge of the boat, I dropped into the water and sunk down, down, down and didn't touch the bottom. I know, that's the ocean for you, but it was still strange.

The dad jumped into the water with us.

"Only two hundred meters," Mr. Kosta called from behind us. "Miss, only two hundred meters."

Now was not a good time for me to convert meters to yards.

We swam to the break in the rock; it was the cave we came to see. We swam in; there were no seals to welcome us. We paddled around for a while and were each surrounded in the most surprising light blue color. We were glowing light blue. We dove and swam and wished we had our cameras. It was like we were plugged in. We laughed at the surprise of being in a "state of blue."

Mr. Kosta helped us climb back into the boat and drove us slowly to the beach. I stayed on the boat, thinking that castle was calling my name. When we got to the dock, Mr. Kosta said, "Fifteen euros."

"Fifteen?" I said, bristling. "No. You said it was ten euros."

He held up three fingers, signaling three people for 15 euros.

He was offering us half price, but how do you say in Greek, I don't know those men and I'm not paying for their boat trip? We did look like a family and now I looked like a cheapskate who refused to pay their way, which truly saddened the captain. In the end he accepted the 10 euros, but he wouldn't look me in the eye.

I was free to explore once more.

I climbed many steps up to the castle where I watched as two men replaced the Greek flag, which they had to wrestle in the wind and keep it from whipping their faces and bodies. The water was so clear that the sea resembled a relief map where different depths showed up in different colors of blue.

I made my way back to town and found the duty-free shop. A man who worked at my hotel wanted a bottle of Jack Daniels whiskey. He gave me cash in euros. And I thought it was funny that I was buying a bottle of cheap whiskey that my friends back home wouldn't drink, from a shop in Greece with my American credit card, for a Turkish friend.

The ferry backed out of the marina and we were returning to Turkey. I looked up at the castle and saw the new Greek flag waving to us from the top of the mountain.

I waved back.

∽

Photo next page: Kızılhisar or the Island of Meis, Greece

DAY 28: KAŞ: SHOPPING

I picked up a pair of shorts in a store in Kaş and considered whether I would wear these shorts at home. Price was not an issue, the shorts cost $5, but I've never subscribed to the "disposable" clothing trend; most of my clothes have been around for years. Were these shorts a beach fling, or would they fit into my wardrobe at home?

As I considered what value I'd give this purchase, I got an uncomfortable feeling that someone was watching me. I looked up and caught the eye of a Turkish man staring at me. He didn't look away when I caught him watching; he intensified his stare.

I was trying to get used to this. The staring. Some men stared. Some women stared. Some children stared. I get it, I'm different, but people stared at me as if they were waiting for me to unzip my skin, turn into a fairy and grant wishes, or something.

My aim in traveling is to be invisible. I'm here to learn and observe, not to flaunt that I'm an American woman traveling alone. I packed clothes for their quick-drying abilities, not their fashion forward fit. My drab clothing choices with limited combination potential ensure that I'm the worst-dressed woman wherever I go.

Back home if a man stared at me this way, I would call security and ask for help; here it's the norm. It's unsettling to be watched, constantly.

A friend of mine was born with a drastic physical deformity. When she goes out, people stare at her as if she's a monster. She finds it tiring to be the object of so much attention. She spends a lot of time with children in schools, teaching them how to scan a room and look at what you want to see without staring.

They could use her sensitivity training here, or it may be time for me to accept that staring is acceptable in Turkey.

Today marks one month that I've been on the road; twenty-eight days of wearing the same three shirts again and again. This lack of selection was a time saver, no doubt: research shows that having fewer choices enables you to dress faster. But the research never points out how tiring the lack of choices can be.

To celebrate being on the road for one month, I stepped into a few clothing stores to have a look around.

There were many clothing shops in Kaş where the owner was the designer and dressmaker. Each shop sported a different style and for the most part the clothes were affordable. I would have loved to pack my suitcase with shirts and dresses and flattering skirts, but these clothes wouldn't work on the travel road.

And I was on the travel road.

I found a store and decided to treat myself to a new shirt and a new pair of shorts. I know, not a giant leap in wardrobe freshening, but I only had one carry-on suitcase and everything I owned had to fit inside.

In Turkey, store attendants prove their attentiveness by following you around the store, waiting to be of service. A worker stands within a few feet of you while you shop. If you slow in front of a red top, he or she leaps to attention and pulls more sizes and colors from the rack and pushes them in front of you so there's no chance you can consider only the red shirt. Add to that the ongoing language barrier and the burden of bargaining; shopping here is not relaxing.

Please stop staring. Let me think.

Shopping back home, you can wander in a store begging for someone to help you open a dressing room or talk about sizing options and at times you wonder if anyone works there. I was at Home Depot recently to look at ceiling tiles and a sign stated, "Need help? Go to our website." Shopping in the States and shopping in Turkey are very different experiences.

I found a dressing room and tried on the shorts and a t-shirt. They had great travel potential. I found a small backpack that I could take on my boat cruise tomorrow. In fact I could wear my new clothes tomorrow, too.

I looked around to see if that man who was watching me earlier would notice that I was buying something. I didn't see him, but there were three women and two other men holding me in hard stares.

I held each piece of clothing up in front of me as if I were considering it before I bought it, so the onlookers could soothe their curiosity.

Larsoy Tours recommended the boat trip. People jump, swim and play around the boat during the full-day tour.

The German family was willing to hike to the very top of the castle with Holly Winter Huppert: friends for life!

DAY 29: KAŞ: BOAT

The boat stopped and I heard a rubbing noise as the anchor dropped. A deckhand dove into the water behind the boat and tied a thick line to an enormous rock. When it comes to steadying a boat, there's nothing like a rope tied to a rock.

A voice announced over the loudspeaker to the seventy people on board, first in Turkish then in English: "We will stop here at this cove for thirty minutes for a swim. Please stay near the boat, there are sharks in the ocean."

After my exciting day trip to Greece, I'd returned to the travel agency to see if the owner could recommend something just as fun. He accepted the challenge, asked me a few questions, and then recommended a group boat trip. Captain Ergon's boat sails to various islands in the sea where you can swim, eat lunch, and at one stop you can walk around and explore ancient ruins.

Ancient ruins? Sold!

After that shark announcement, I didn't want to stay near the boat, I wanted to stay *on* the boat. Prepositions matter when you're talking about sharks. I swam next to a baby shark years ago when I was swimming off the Galapagos Islands. I was safe, but my mind worked overtime. What if. What if.

Any trepidation about marine animals with sharp teeth dissipated when I looked out at that blue, blue water. It looked like someone added too much blueberry Kool-Aid to the punch. If I swam in blue water, would I turn blue? If my skin turned blue, would I rather join the Blue Man Group or become a Smurf?

It's good to have choices while riding on a three-story boat under a shade covering, lounging on a thick cushion along the Turquoise Coast of Turkey.

The mom from the German family sitting next to me waved me forward, inviting me to join her family for a dip in the Mediterranean. It was ninety degrees out; I was ready for a swim.

You know how a baby's cradle rocks back and forth in a predictable way? Well, a boat rolls up and forward and back and there's no way to anticipate the movements. We stumbled across the upstairs deck, grabbing at the "Holding Rope" above our heads and trying to remain upright as we wobbled to the stairs.

I climbed down the narrow orange steps to the first floor, then climbed down a ladder into the cold, swishing, salty water. I swam in liquid blue. Okay, the water wasn't that cold. I could see the bottom of the sea in our shallow cove; there were giant boulders under me, and I wondered what was under them.

The mom decided to stay on the boat, which is like inviting someone to the fair and then refusing to go. Hello? Her husband and children tried to get her into the water, but she wasn't interested. Since I just met her I don't know if she was the kind of person who would send me into the ocean before her to scare away the sharks, or feed them, or perhaps she was hoping I would organize shark rides.

I was ready for a workout and I did swim for a bit, but then became distracted with the color of the water and floated around with minimal effort because of that high salt concentration. Floating beats swimming any day.

I settled on my mat when the boat moved on and used my translate app to talk to the German family lounging next to me. I told the mom and her 8th-grade daughter that I knew one German phrase, because my mother used to say it to us when we were children.

They waited while I dug it out of my memory. How did she say it again?

"Mach schnell!"

The mom laughed and pantomimed that she said it to her daughter all the time. The daughter nodded quickly in agreement.

It was time to add more sunscreen. We slathered. We sprayed. We dripped sunscreen onto our bodies and rubbed it in. The mom pointed to my back.

"Yes. Please."

One of the things I can't do as a solo traveler is apply sunscreen to my back.

The boat stopped at another swim location. This time the mom swam and so did the 10th-grade sister and the dad.

And so the day progressed. We napped when the boat moved and swam when it stopped. Lunch was an unexpected feast: a buffet with whole grilled fish, salads, vegetable dishes and desserts. I sat with my German friends and talked to the 10th-grade girl in English.

She told me about a book she was reading in school. I had to ask her the title three different times; I'd never heard of it, but thought I would look it up when I got back to Wi-Fi, because I was curious as to what books teachers in Frankfurt assigned to high school students, but I lost the slip of paper I wrote the title on.

After another nap and swim combination we arrived at the island, where we could walk around for a while. The boat would sail again in one hour. The German family and I followed a path that was lined with craftspeople selling things made from shells and beads and flowy material.

We stopped to pose in front of a king's tomb. It was a beautiful place to be buried, just on the edge of the water.

We were ready to find the old castle on top of the hill. We climbed the narrow stone stairs. It was hot and around every turn there were more steps. We were hiking away from the dock. The view was great; I could see out to sea. Nope, no pirate ships.

I imagined watching the ferry set sail from that faraway vantage point. We only had an hour. I didn't think I could make it as a shell jeweler.

We climbed and climbed and stopped to catch our breath, then climbed some more. Just one more set of stairs and we reached the castle. We stood, panting at the outer wall feeling accomplished, then had to climb another set of stairs to get to the first level, and several more sets of stairs to reach the very top, where the wind blew and the views were the best.

The people who lived there long ago must have had the strongest legs. I bet they could sprint up to the castle on a moment's notice to attend a feast or a slumber party. Standing there at the top, I understood why the king built his tomb at sea level so that in his death there would be no stairs, just smooth sailing. I wondered where the queen's tomb was.

The island is known for their handmade ice cream. The dad treated us all. I got the mulberry; it was creamier than other ice creams I'd had in Turkey and had more natural fruit flavor. I considered moving to the island to eat this ice cream every day, but thought the stairs would depress me over time.

Down. We climbed back to the boat and resumed our napping positions as the boat moved us to yet another swimming location. And no matter how tired I was, even when I felt a chill from that constant wind, I couldn't say no to swimming in that blue, blue water.

When the boat anchored again, I floated behind it and took in the view. People jumped off the boat. People swam. People snorkeled. People raced. Children held plastic noodles and floated between family members.

The contrast between the blue water and the white rocks along the islands and the greenest trees dazzled me.

I tuned in to myself. What a lovely day on a lovely boat surrounded by lovely people. The water was choppier than it was earlier.

Wait. I was no longer next to the boat. Wait, how did that happen? I was more than a hundred yards away from safety; I was floating out to sea.

This was a problem. The islands around me were unpopulated and though I'd enjoyed reading the book, *The Swiss Family Robinson* as a child, I didn't think I could catch fish with my hands.

I turned towards the boat, hoping there was a lookout on board who would send a lifeboat for me. No lookout. Nobody noticed that I was missing; I was on my own, which meant if I couldn't make it back to the boat, then I would learn how to catch fish with my hands.

After kicking my feet as hard as I could and using my best overhand power swim, I barely moved forward. It was as if my anchor were down. Defying the tide, I pushed my body towards the boat and swam as hard as I could, then stopped to rest while the tide pulled me backwards, erasing any progress.

There was probably a trick for swimming against an outgoing current, but there was no way to research that skill while swimming. Shame, I would have welcomed the information. I swam harder and thought about how lucky I was that there weren't any sharks, which made me worry that there might be sharks, which helped power my drive.

Eventually I did make it back and it was like a game of hide-and-go-seek where the "seekers" stopped playing the game, the "hider" wasn't missed. The same crowd played around the boat, swimming, jumping, splashing young children, and didn't notice how I was red-faced and panting when I climbed onboard.

I found my way to my towel and lay gasping for air while the mother, who was also out of breath, spoke in rapid German while she pointed to herself and then pointed out to sea. She made fast swimming motions.

I pantomimed that the same thing happened to me. She understood.

I wanted to ask her if she knew how to catch fish with her hands, but it didn't really matter anymore.

It was snack time. I accepted the chocolate bar and stared out into the most beautiful blue water I'd ever seen.

Holly—1. Sharks—0.

Ready for our water fight against 4 other Jeeps. Holly Winter Huppert is the fourth from the left.

Holly Winter Huppert washes off her clay mask.

DAY 30: KAŞ: WATER FIGHT

I climbed into the back of an open-air Jeep and sat on a bench that ran down the side. There were nine other people back there, all of us squished onto the benches. Two more people sat up front with the guide; I was the only non-Turkish person on the trip.

The guide smiled at me and said, "Don't worry, Olly, I yell you everything in English when we go restaurant."

I thanked him and smiled at the people around me so they might know I was a friendly sort.

What exactly did the owner of the travel agency mean when he said that I wouldn't like this trip?

Sitting in the back of a Jeep was like sitting across the table from strangers at a long dinner table, but without the table. We smiled at each other.

When I told the travel agency that I had used several times in Kaş that I wanted to take a Jeep tour, the owner told me I wouldn't like it. His son said that I'd probably like the canyon part.

It was only for a day and I was open for trying something out of my comfort zone, but sitting in the back of an open Jeep without a seatbelt was already out of my comfort zone. We left the city and rode into the mountains. The guide drove and turned up the music. Turkish music. The other women in my group sang along.

At the restaurant, the guide told me that he'd explain it in Turkish, first, and I figured that was fair since I was in Turkey, you know, native language first. He spoke rapidly and I watched the faces of the group as he spoke. At first they listened, as if it were a lecture: heads turned up, concentrating on the information.

Then they started to register a little unease at what they were hearing, they tilted their heads forward and opened their mouths a little. They looked at each other and stared wide eyed, as if the talk the guide had just given was upsetting.

The guide looked at me and said in English, "You getting all this, right, Olly?"

I laughed, "Not quite."

When he finished, the others in my group looked at each other. What was the look on their faces, disbelief?

After their ten-minute chat, the guide pulled up a chair and sat next to me. "We going water fight. You have water balloons five lira and water gun ten lira. After the fight, we go to gorge and walk and then lunch."

Not that I was holding a stopwatch or anything, but it seemed that my orientation was about 9-1/2 minutes shorter than theirs. I wondered what I missed.

He left the group, and we ate breakfast and drank tea and a woman and her husband spoke to me in English, and then translated for the others.

She was a psychologist and he was a social worker. We compared stories about working with special education students. They told me about their system of education and how students with learning needs get no specialized services or learning plans. I told them that my country did a good job of caring for students with disabilities.

Two of the couples were on their honeymoon, and two more had been together for years. Three women were traveling together which made twelve of us altogether.

Where are you from? And where are you from? What do you do?

And what do you do? Is this your first time to Turkey? Which part of Turkey are you from?

I bought a bag of water balloons and told my guide that I didn't think I needed a super soaker, because I was a good twenty years older than the others on this trip and because I have terrible aim.

"You will be sorry," he said. "You need it."

We packed our belongings into large plastic bags, tied the tops closed and put them in the front of the Jeep on the passenger seat.

Go time.

There were four five-gallon buckets filled with water on the floor in the back, and our water balloon purchases lined the seats. There was no room to sit. There was no room to stand. I turned to the guide, awaiting direction.

The guide told us we were going to stand, anyway, so don't worry about the seats being full of water balloons.

So now we were going to stand in the back of the Jeep while it zips along back-country roads?

The guide whispered to me in English, "The secret this: save balloons for end or we run out water."

One of the other guides picked up a hose and sprayed our group as if we were parched flowers. We squealed in communal discomfort, and the hose found a new target in one of the other four or five Jeeps all filled with people; everyone got a shower.

I pointed to the Jeep across the lot and said to the psychologist, "I think that is our enemy." There were only four people inside and they looked meek and a little afraid.

The psychologist said, "If that is our enemy, we will win."

The guide started our vehicle and drove along a paved road. This was a little town up in the mountains with no discernable business district; there was little or no traffic. We stood in the back and I used my brute strength to clutch the rails that ran along the sides so I might steady myself.

At first I thought we were going to ride to a field where we would have an epic water fight. But within moments, I realized that the water fight would be from the Jeep while we stood clutching the sides and racing down a mountain road. Our opponents were the people in the four other Jeeps.

Remember when the owner of the travel agency said I wouldn't like this? I hoped there was room in the front seat next to the driver.

There wasn't a lot of room for my feet because all twelve of us were back there and those buckets of water took up a lot of room. The driver pulled into the oncoming traffic lane that had no traffic and pulled alongside another Jeep.

It was an example of learning on the go. Our group doused the occupants of the other Jeep with super soakers and they returned fire. I used every bit of my strength to hold on, understanding now why the rails were cushioned and how having a super soaker might have protected me from direct hits.

Every part of me dripped water.

The guide swerved the Jeep and we all fell into each other, laughing and helping each other up.

He swerved on purpose, to make us fall while driving 40–50 miles per hour? Likely the company running this trip didn't have any insurance policies for guests.

The water fight continued. I forgot about wanting to sit up front.

We passed small villages. Some locals watched the water fights from afar as we sped by, others stood at the side of the roadway, picked up hoses and showered us with cold mountain water.

Yeah? I see how you are: it's on! We did our best to return fire, but a super soaker doesn't stand up to a water hose.

The road became a series of turns. We continued speeding along, moving from one lane to the other lane so we could spray our opponents with water.

The woman in the yellow skirt gave me her water gun, "Don't need," and began launching balloons. I filled the gun from the bucket of water next to my feet and shot the water at a group of strangers in another Jeep. Not to boast, but I think I got every person in that Jeep wet, including the driver.

There may have been a rule about not soaking the driver that I missed at orientation. The driver shook his head at me. I shrugged in an "I don't speak Turkish" kind of way.

Our guide slammed on the brakes, and we all fell over like dominoes. As we scrambled to right ourselves, he got out of the Jeep and picked up something from the road. What was it, a turtle? Money? A can of beans?

A water balloon, unbroken.

He threw it into the center of our group, and it spattered in such a way, we all got wetter. I thought that he might have a lot of experience when it comes to water balloon fights.

And we were off again. Defending. Dousing. Dripping.

Two eight-year-old boys waved hoses and wet us all. We sprayed them back and were then on the lookout for more locals joining in the fun.

"Look at that man," I shouted to my comrades about a man standing next to the road. "He has a bucket of water. Get him!" But nobody caught my English, so the man threw the water on us, but remained dry due to our poor strategizing skills.

When a Jeep snuck up on the left side and my group was preoccupied shooting water out the right side and didn't see them, I yelled, "Incoming, left side!" but they didn't understand that, either.

We got wetter.

Slowly we became a team. Tapping each other and pointing towards any group that got too close.

The floor of the Jeep was wet. I was wet. The sun beat down on my face and arms and hands. Was my sunscreen rated for how effective it is when gallons and gallons of water are dumped over you for a forty-minute period?

That's a long water fight: forty minutes while standing in a swerving, speeding Jeep.

You know how big corporations have "Team Building" days? Well, this was more effective. We stopped apologizing when we fell on someone else as strangers became friends. We were in this together. It wasn't about picking a leader or communicating a strategy, we were all in 100 percent, in charge of our common objective: get everyone else wet. Period. That's all we had to do.

In time we figured out why there were liter bottles of water scattered along the seats; we emptied them into the buckets, and may

I mention here that even pouring a liter of water into a bucket from the back of a speeding vehicle is more difficult than you'd imagine?

There were two little boys holding a bucket. I shouted an alarm and tapped the shoulders of the people around me, "Look!" My team mobilized; we doused the kids.

While we showered them with water, I got a good look in their bucket. Grapes. It was filled with grapes. Grapes? There was no water. They weren't joining the game; they were trying to make some money.

The kids probably woke at dawn and picked grapes so they could sell them and make extra money for school supplies, or something. We were moving too fast to see the expression on their faces when we slobbered them with cold water, but I fear we may have squashed their entrepreneurial spirit.

For life.

We threw water balloons at the other groups and sometimes they burst on contact, and when I happened to be the one throwing the balloon, I felt like I'd won the lottery. Major score.

You must understand, this whole scenario is far from my typical way of having a good time. Last summer my sister-in-law had a party at a racetrack where friends and family rented specialized go-carts and raced around a professional track. The "cars" would go over 40 miles per hour and the drivers had to wear seatbelts and helmets.

I wasn't invited to the party and heard about it later. My brother said, "You would have hated it."

I agreed with him and was glad I wasn't invited.

But here I was barreling down a mountain road, in a foreign country, in the back of a speeding vehicle while doing every possible grab to hold my balance. To shoot a super soaker, you can't hold on at the same time. To fill the super soaker, you can't hold on at the same time.

I didn't have a seatbelt or a helmet, and there were no waivers to sign. Heck, the tour company didn't even have my phone number or country of residence. Did they know my last name?

I know. This model wouldn't work in the States.

When it was over, we were all a little sad. Really, was that forty minutes?

Our guide locked our stuff in a room, then took us to a gorge. He showed us a bowl of clay and told us it was good for our skin. We coated our faces with the thick, gooey mud, and I put on a second coat, thinking it might cool the sunburn I expected for spending time in the direct sun without reapplying sunscreen.

We posed for pictures with mud on our faces.

"Smile first," the guide commanded from behind his cell phone. Snap. Snap. Snap.

"Now look afraid." Snap. Snap. Snap.

It cost 10 lira ($1.20) to buy special water shoes and we walked down two hundred steps to get to the water level. What a beautiful place. The water flowed over rocks that made mini-waterfalls and rushed by. It was the kind of place you'd love to have a picnic next to. The guide was carrying an umbrella, but it didn't look like rain. Must be something else I missed in the orientation.

First we posed for pictures. The guide had us stand under a steady stream of water and smile into the camera while we still had the mud on our faces.

When it was my turn, I stood under the stream of water and registered shock and pain at the same time: Cold water. Hard water. This hurt. It was like putting your head under a jackhammer.

Snap. Snap. Snap. "Okay, Olly," he said. "Now wash you face from clay."

Next up: the waterfall.

Our job was to walk up the river, but there were no sidewalks alongside, and nobody had thought to build a boardwalk over the top so we might climb in our bare feet if we wanted to. No. For this part of our day, we needed to climb up the river from inside the river.

Those cute little rocks became stumbling blocks. The water was cold. The rocks, slippery.

Sometimes I crawled, other times I stepped. At times the water was up to my knees, other times it was ankle deep. Every time I climbed through one area there was a turn in the river and there was more climbing to do. It's like rock scrambling, but from inside the river.

The prize at the top of the river was a waterfall that crashed down from the cliffs above. It was magnificent.

There was a stump in front of the waterfall and the guide commanded us to stand on it, each person or couple, for more photos.

Look at the waterfall. Snap. Look at me. Snap. Arms up. Snap. Here, hold this umbrella. Snap.

The only way to get out of the canyon was to walk out the way we came in, through the river. As I knocked my shins and feet against boulders, the cool water temperature acted like a giant ice pack.

On we climbed, as our guide shouted encouragement in two languages until we made it back to the Jeep.

We drove to the other part of the gorge and I got a history lesson along the way. Earthquake. Gorge. I'm pretty sure the group got a longer lesson, but I was happy with the basics.

Climbing in the river here was more difficult, the water moved faster and was a lot colder, about forty degrees. Welcome water shoes.

My feet asked if we had to worry about hypothermia, since the water was so cold, and I told them to stop whining.

We posed for photos here, too. While sitting in the water. While sitting in the 40-degree cold water. While sitting in the 40-degree cold water with more water rushing over us. One at a time, we did our puppet master's bidding.

"Sit lower," the guide called out. "Move closer to the waterfall. Lower. Sit up more. Smile." Snap. Snap. Snap.

I learned something about myself; isn't that why we travel, to know ourselves better? I learned that when sitting in 40-degree water, I cannot smile. I cannot breathe. I cannot look at the camera. And although there are no big creatures in the water, if you look at my photograph where I'm sitting in this water, it looks like an alligator was eating my foot.

As we climbed out of this river, if one of us found sure footing, a hand was held out for the next person to help get them over a bump.

They should rename this trip the "Water Challenge."

We got our belongings and walked to the restaurant for our prepaid lunch. Buffet food. Good food. Meze. Fish. Chicken. Cooked greens. Many more cooked veggies. We broke into groups, and removed our shoes and sat at low tables on cushions, and ate while we took turns in the hammock that swung between us.

Why don't we have restaurants like this at home?

We had a ride through the ruins of Patara, and I decided there was no bad way to look at ruins, but riding past them in the back of a Jeep was more than acceptable.

We ended the day at Kaputas beach. The twelve of us walked to the shady end of the beach, put down our towels and walked into the sea. We swam. We floated. We watched people climb the rocks next to the sign that said "Climbing rocks forbidden. Jumping forbidden." And watched as young people jumped into the water.

I thought about climbing the rocks and jumping into the sea.

But I didn't.

DAY 31: KONYA: UNCOMFORTABLE

A man in a blue shirt stopped me and said, "Taxi?"

In New York you would never talk to a stranger at the bus station, then I remembered: in Turkey there are plainclothes workers in bus stations. I had twenty minutes to get through the bus station security, find the ticket counter, buy a ticket, and find my next bus in a center that was as big as an airport.

"Konya," I said. "Bus. Konya."

He walked and I followed behind him. Past ticket counters. Past vendors selling trinkets. Past food stalls.

Food? Oh, I was ready for some food. There was a power outage at the hotel in Kaş when I was packing. The only window in the room was small, there was no way I could pack in the dark. No way. By the time the lights came back on I had only minutes to spare, which meant no breakfast and no time to buy snacks.

It was my least favorite hotel on the whole trip. The owner was warm and chatty with others, but unfriendly with me. I had looked for her the day before I was departing, to be sure the room was paid through the internet company I had booked it on, but she told me she was too busy to talk.

The morning I was leaving I tried to find her. She was on the phone in her office. I said, "All good?"

She waved me away, which made me think it must be good.

I didn't like my room, either. It was a giant box with only one tiny window that was next to the rooster's cage. The air conditioner was broken, so it was so cold in the room, I had to step outside to warm up.

Buses in Turkey seem to leave the station at least five minutes early. They are unapologetic about this change in schedule; when they feel there are enough people on the bus, they leave.

I made the first bus with minutes to spare, but the only food rations I had with me were two bags of roasted almonds. Good thing I like almonds.

The man in a blue shirt at the next bus station in Antalya walked me down two different hallways to a ticket booth behind another wall. He interrupted six men who were deep in conversation, insisting that they sell me a bus ticket right away, my bus was leaving in fifteen minutes.

I thanked the man for helping me.

He nodded his understanding and walked away.

My four-hour bus from Kaş to Antalya cost me 30 lira (under $4). This next ticket from Antalya to Konya cost 80 lira ($10). I didn't care about the price, but worried that this trip was longer than the four hours I expected it to be. Why was this ride more than double the cost?

The ticket agent handed me my ticket and told me where to get the bus, in Turkish. When I got outside, I said to the first person I saw, "Konya?"

He pointed to a bus that had the words, "Super Batman" written across the front. Batman is the name of a small city in the southeast part of Turkey; the city wasn't on my list of places to visit. I would get off the bus in Konya; the bus would continue to Batman.

Really? I smiled. A Bat-mo-bus? I giggled, imagining the superhero Batman running a bus company.

I showed the ticket to a young man who stood outside the bus wearing a blue shirt with the words, "Super Batman" on it. I didn't take his picture, but I really, really wanted to.

The young man treated me like a slimeball that hadn't showered in six months. He reluctantly took my suitcase and waved me onto the bus. Okay. No problem, Mr. Impatient Turkish Man. You are but a small part of my travels, so you can cop all the attitude you want.

I found my seat by searching for the tiny numbers printed on the outside armrest, #26, and sat down. I had a window seat, which is always a good thing, and also had control of the curtain that covers the window. If it were too sunny, I could close the curtain. If the sun went behind a cloud, I could open the curtain. Having control of the curtain is a powerful position on a bus.

The young man came on the bus and shook his head at me and pointed to a different seat towards the back. I tried to show him my ticket with the number, which annoyed him even more. I got another window seat with curtain privileges.

Okay. No problem. I don't really care where I sit.

Slowly the bus filled with people. A family got on, there must have been fifteen of them. The women wore head scarves and long sleeves and long pants, and the men told the women and children where to sit. They were a happy family, laughing and joking around, and they had bags and bags of food that they placed in the compartment over the seats.

Well, they were happy until they saw me. Maybe they knew I was low on food and they didn't want to share their provisions? A man from the group sat next to me and frowned as he asked me questions about where I was from and where I was going.

I knew the man was disrespecting me; a man doesn't sit next to a woman who isn't in his family, but I didn't know why.

He got on his phone and called someone and shouted into the phone in Turkish.

Something about America and New York. I didn't think it was a welcome message.

The young man who checked my ticket earlier came to get me and moved me to the front seat of the bus next to a little girl who might have been eight years old. Her mother sat behind her and protested in a loud, arguing voice, but the young man held up his hand and she quieted.

I got the message and made myself as small as I could.

The little girl sat frozen in her seat, staring straight ahead. I hated making her feel uncomfortable.

I napped and napped some more. Traveling is when I catch up on my sleep.

Several hours into the ride, I needed the bathroom. There wasn't one onboard. My first bus of the day stopped every hour for a quick bathroom break. I was too scared to jump off and go, until the bus stopped for gas. Surely, I could find a bathroom and use it and make it back out before the bus refueled.

Yes, it worked. I made it into the center, found the bathroom and was back on the bus before it gassed up.

But that was a few hours ago. The bus driver and the young man drank water and tea and coffee nonstop. Surely, they must need the bathroom, too?

I took out my roasted almonds, opened them and offered them to the little girl in the next seat. She reached her tiny hand into the bag, got a handful of nuts, and pulled them out slowly and ate one nut at a time.

I would never have offered food to a child at home without asking the parents first, but here people offer food to those around them. Likely shelled nuts were a rare treat for her. I tried to share them with the mother and her siblings sitting behind us, but the mother stuck out her chin and shook her head.

Okay.

Three and a half hours into the bus ride we pulled into a center. This had to be a rest stop. Many people got off the bus, some got their suitcases. Some walked away. I found the young worker and said, "Toilet?" and pointed to myself.

He shook his head no and held up three fingers.

Really? This is a three-minute stop?

I went back on the bus and sat in my seat. More people got off the bus.

I found the worker again and said, "Toilet?""

He nodded his head, " Yes," slowly as if I were developmentally delayed.

It was my first squat toilet of the trip and was fancier than some I've seen in the past: this toilet had a drain flap. There was a faucet in the stall with a red plastic pitcher that was already filled with water. Okay. Got it. After you go, wash the toilet out with the water. Then refill the pitcher with clean water for the next person.

You know how bathroom floors are unsanitary? Well, in a bathroom with a squat toilet, the floor is always wet, and you hope it's from the spigot spraying clean water.

I got back to the bus and everyone was gone. No driver. No worker. No passengers. It's as if all the people were abducted. My bag was untouched on the front seat, so I walked around the center some more. Lots of boxed candies and food stalls with fried foods. Nothing I could eat here, even if I had the time.

I watched as the bus next to ours pulled out. Wouldn't it be a sad twist of fate if my suitcase made it to Konya and I didn't?

I returned to the bus and sat. And waited. And sat. In the end I think the three fingers the worker held up were meant to signify thirty minutes. I wanted to give him a list of ways to show thirty minutes the next time he had a foreigner, like ten fingers flashed three times. Or three fingers on one hand and a big zero with the other hand? Or could he have written down the number when he saw I was confused?

When the young worker returned to the bus, he nodded to me with a sad expression on his face. Wait, was that a look of—pity?

After a few minutes he served drinks. I asked for *su*: water. He couldn't understand. "Water," I said. "Su." He shrugged.

The little girl next to me spoke quietly to the man and I heard her say "su" and a word that would rhyme with water, "vater" several times in a quiet voice. She held him in an innocent stare, then repeated that I wanted water until the man gave in and handed me a water.

A little girl standing up to a rude man. Her courage warmed me.

After a while I asked her if she spoke English. She shook her head no. I opened the bag of nuts, and she reached her whole hand into the bag and took a handful and ate each nut slowly, and then accepted another handful.

When we arrived in Konya six hours after we started the trip, the young worker came to my seat and pointed to me and said, "Konya."

I thanked him.

Before I left, I looked the girl in the eye and said a heartfelt, "Thank you."

"You're welcome," she said.

I smiled big. She must have practiced that phrase in her head while we were riding along. She didn't say "velcome" as many Turkish speakers say. She got the "W" sound in there.

"Check you out," I said, quietly. "You got the "w" sound in there. Well done."

She smiled and nodded yes this time. The sentiment was understood.

The taxi to the hotel was easy. I arrived to a welcoming man who spoke wonderful English. He upgraded my room to one that had three handmade carpets on the floor.

An oasis in travel.

Rumi's tomb.

The Whirling Dervishes spin as a way to be closer to God.

DAY 32: KONYA: RUMI

I texted my friend Amy, who was traveling in Europe with her husband. I wrote, "My data plan for Google Fi died in Turkey. No translate program. No more internet. Why? Why?"

She texted back questions about customer support.

I texted her again; she was the one who recommended the plan that gave free international calling. "No support. No sympathy. But I found a small phone store with a team of men who sold me a SIMS card for Turkey. I can't text friends and family, but I can use the internet, the GPS and the translation program."

I asked about her next travel steps. She told me about a possible airline strike on the very flight they booked, and wrote that they were going to spend time in a part of France they already knew and loved.

She texted me, asking about what happened to the photos from my "Water" story. I texted back about how losing electricity at my last hotel put me behind schedule and messed with my uploads. I hadn't had time to fix it.

I heard an announcement in the theater where I sat but ignored it. I was a half hour early for the dance program I'd come to see. They'd probably announce the information again in a little while.

When I'd checked in to my hotel (Konya Dervish Hotel), I asked the owners about the whirling dervishes, monks with specialized training who dance to connect to God. I searched for times and places, but the information online was difficult, if not impossible, to find. The mother of the family I stayed with in Selçuk called her mother, who lives in Konya. Her mother said that my information was correct. The dervishes danced on Saturday nights at 7:30.

Okay. Good. I arranged my entire Turkey travel schedule to be sure I would be in Konya for a Saturday night performance.

When I checked in, I asked the owner's brother, to be sure. Did it start at 7:30 as I'd read? Where was the best place to sit in the theater? Was it safe to walk to the hotel after, or should I take a taxi? What time should I arrive if I wanted a very good seat?

The brother answered my questions and said I could get there by 7:00, so I decided to be there by 6:45. I'd come all this way and didn't want to miss out on the performance. No. Matter. What.

Google was correct in telling me I could walk there in ten minutes. I arrived at the outer edge of the property in ten minutes, but the Mevlâna Kültür Merkezi is as big as a stadium: I had a lot more walking to do before I found a seat.

I followed the brother's advice and walked to the back of the round theater so I could see the musicians and the dancers. I sat behind a man in a white cap who looked like a spiritual man, and worried I could distract him with the many photos I wanted to take.

I wanted to remember this performance.

I first heard about the thirteenth-century Persian Sufi poet and mystic, Rumi, who is also known as Mevlâna, twenty-five years ago when I was an assistant manager of a Walden Bookstore. At the time I was dealing with another medical zinger that had attached itself to me and wouldn't let go. In order to deal with the onslaught of medical trauma, I moved away from home and found a place where I could heal. Dothan, Alabama was the perfect place to land.

As the assistant manager of a bookstore, I had lots of time to browse the shelves. I found a Rumi book in the poetry section, bought it and read every poem several times; they were easy to read but packed a punch.

I copied his poem, "Guest House," and carried it in my wallet for years. Later when I taught high school, I made my students memorize it.

The owner of the hotel talked about Rumi with me during breakfast this morning. He was surprised at the intensity of my love of his poetry and we got into a philosophical discussion about the poet.

He told me about Konya and its place in the medical world, the whirling dervishes, and what we know now about Rumi. He said the poet was underestimated for centuries (that's a lot of underestimation), and that he was a trained medical doctor who believed words could heal.

There is so much to love about Rumi.

After breakfast I went to the Mevlâna Museum, which is Rumi's mausoleum (where he's buried) and also the dervish lodge of the Mevlevi Order, where the whirling dervishes studied, back when Rumi was alive. The museum houses a series of small rooms with displays of writings and clothing and other things that belonged to the mystic.

The crowds were there to see the displays. I wasn't the only one who traveled from far away to see this museum; people came from all over Turkey to spend time to learn more about the poet.

One room housed Rumi's tomb. It takes some getting used to the fact that tombs can be inside, in the States we keep our dead people outside in cemeteries. But here the tombs of important dead people can be housed inside any number of mosques or holy places.

Rumi's tomb was by far the most beautifully decorated place I'd seen so far in the country, with decorative tile and tapestry surrounding it. People walked by and whispered prayers under their breath, posed for photos and stood taking in the beauty.

I was deeply moved by the museum and found myself on the verge of tears the whole time I was there, but I wasn't sure why. Was I connecting this place to a time in my life where I was running from illnesses? Or was I feeling grateful for the words that helped me heal?

Or was there a kind of "energy" in the space that made it feel like home? I couldn't explain why, but in looking at the calligraphy writings and the old clothes and the various instruments, it was as if I had seen them before. I tried to stay open to the feelings without naming them, as Rumi suggests in his writing.

When my Turkish friends asked about my plans for seeing as much of Turkey as I could, each asked, "Konya? Why Konya? Not Konya..."

"Whirling dervishes," I'd say, but nobody understood until I got to the hotel. The owner understood my pilgrimage, and so did the man who volunteered at the gift shop in the museum because he loves to be around people who love Mevlâna.

So getting to the whirling dervishes early was a top priority. I sat in the theater, texting Amy. There were so many things on my mind. The last hotel I stayed at in Kaş had just sent me a message saying that I didn't pay for the room.

"What?" I messaged the hotel in Kaş. "I booked and paid by the internet."

"This never happened before," she texted me. "You must send me your credit card numbers right away."

Um, no.

I'd been going over my online banking orders searching for the charge, perhaps there was a snafu and I didn't pay.

I had a lot on my mind.

At 7:00 the theater quieted. The dancers walked out onto the stage area. Wait, they're starting now? A full half hour early?

See? That's why I like to arrive early.

The dervishes walked into the arena wearing black capes over their white clothes. I sat on the edge of my seat, watching. I've yearned to see this program for more than thirty years.

Audience members were still walking in. Babies cried. People talked and children climbed over the seat backs.

But the dervishes went through their opening with great devotion. Their hats looked like giant thimbles. They sat. They bowed to their leader. They prayed. They stood and walked to a beat, bowing again to the leader.

For a half hour these men moved about the stage area. At 7:30 they took off their capes and began to whirl.

This is it. This is what I wanted to see.

They spun in circles. Hands up. Head leaning to the side. They spun in place. Around and around. Man, I would get dizzy if I did that.

I would trip and fall if I spun around like that. I watched their feet, they stepped to the side, then spun on that foot. Again. Again. Again.

I took photos. I took videos.

The man sitting in front of me who looked spiritual, as he was dressed all in white, took a selfie with the dancing in the background.

The spinning stopped. The dancers walked to the beat of the music, slowly, slowly in a circle. Everything was about the circle. They bowed to their leader, again. They listened to the music.

That ancient flute music was very calming.

After a few minutes, the spinning started again. Around. Around. Around. The stage area filled with the flowing skirts of the men as they spun and spun and spun. They held their arms up in the air and their heads bent to one side. They were completely self-absorbed.

They didn't look anyone in the eye. They didn't look to the audience for attention or reinforcement. I don't think they were worrying about whether they owed money to the last hotel they stayed at.

The extended family next to me talked to each other. Their children ran up and down the steps next to where I sat. They laughed at something funny someone said.

I wondered if the dervishes were annoyed at the lack of respect from some people in the audience. I looked at their faces as they spun to see if I could tell what they were thinking. Peace. Joy. Radiance. I'm mostly sure that they had no idea there were people in the audience.

When I tuned out the people around me, I was able to tune in to the dance floor. I tried to pick my favorite dancer, but the only identifying characteristics were how they bent their heads to the side and how they held their arms up. Some were bent more than others.

Every dancer had a little smile on his face. Every dancer twirled. Every dancer was very focused on the dance and not on the other people in the room.

You know how if you see someone grieving, you feel sad, or if someone is laughing you feel some of that joy? Watching these holy men twirl and spin while in religious ecstasy rubbed off on me. I felt lighter.

I thought I was at the performance to watch other people feel something, but slowly feelings of connection woke inside of me. I felt an increasing joy move through my body. I went from being a viewer to being a participant.

I stopped taking photos and watched.

I thought about how we have that phrase, "Spinning in circles" that we use when we're feeling stressed and ineffective at getting things done.

And as I watched them some more, I thought that getting nothing done should be the goal. Maybe we should spin in circles when we're stressed so that the weight of the world flings off our shoulders.

For their last whirling dance, the men made the same sound we all make when we're stressed: "Ahhh." They danced and called out and spun and called out.

And for some reason their release of burdens removed my burdens, too. Not just the problems of the day, but something deeper was removed. I think a door was opened so that something inside of me could receive more light.

When it was over, I stayed in my seat a while longer, feeling glued in lightness. I wanted to keep this feeling. Bottle it. Wear it as a necklace. Hold it tightly.

I looked around the theater. Most people had left to shop for souvenirs. The theater was nearly empty, but there were a few others riveted to their seats just like I was. They stared at the stage as if the performance were still going on.

It was as if those men had danced into my mind and they were still there, waking up my God connection.

And for this I was deeply grateful.

~

Photo next page: Mevlâna Museum, or Rumi Museum

An archaeologist works at the Boncuklu mound outside of Konya, Turkey near the village of Hayıroğlu.

Artifacts are sorted on a round tray.

DAY 33A: KONYA: DIG

A young archaeologist, under 40 years old with her hair pulled back into a fast ponytail, bent low over her work at the Boncuklu mound outside of Konya, Turkey near the village of Hayıroğlu. She held a bit of plastic over a dirt area and squeezed it in her hand, which produced a puff of air that moved the smallest bit of dust from the place she was studying. Puff.

She bent closer to inspect what was under that bit of dust that moved, then puffed the next grains of sand out of the way. Puff. Study. Puff. Study.

She took a spoon and lifted the bits of sand she had moved and placed them into a bucket, explaining to me that the soil would be examined in a laboratory to find out more information about the people who lived here over 10,000 years ago.

I couldn't fathom anything older than Izmir that logged in at 8,000 years old. Older than Izmir? Getting a personal invitation to visit my first archaeological dig was so exciting that I had trouble sleeping last night.

I'd met Angie, an archaeologist from Australia, when she was visiting the owner of my hotel in Konya. Angie had retired from archaeology years ago and flew here from Australia to join in volunteer digs for several months at a time. After my asking her a lot of questions about the dig, she invited me to see the work for myself.

Really? I could visit?

The owner of my hotel laughed at my enthusiasm and said he would drive and be my guide, I only had to pay the gas.

Seriously?

A professor from Liverpool, England discovered the mound in 2001 and has led digs since then. I met the professor and told him that I knew one of his former students, the archaeologist I stayed with in Selçuk.

The professor smiled warmly and asked how I knew the archaeologist, then before I could answer, said he was very busy and would talk to me later.

Of course.

My guide and I walked over to the second mound where another international team dug. An archaeologist held a spade and dug very slowly. She explained that this soil would not be tested. I nodded as if I understood. Right. Some soil is tested, other soil is not tested.

It is believed that the ancient people who lived in this mound were the first people in Turkey to give up their nomadic life and start a Neolithic Revolution, where they stopped hunting and gathering and began farming. I wondered if they consider people like me, who don't farm but buy everything from farmers, a different revolution?

We found Angie sitting under yet another tent. She leaned over a table and sorted very small objects that had been bagged and saved years ago. She'd sorted the findings into categories on a round, metal plate and pointed out her findings to me: small animal bones, fish bones, bits of pottery, beads and the category that surprised me the most, eggshells.

"You're saying that these two tiny bits of matter are ten-thousand-year-old eggshells? Do we need to rethink composting if eggshell fragments never decompose?"

I volunteered my kindergarten students to help sort the bags and bags of small bits into categories, telling her that children love to sort.

Angie said, "What a great idea, get the children to help!"

"They won't get the categories right," I said, "but they'll try."

We laughed.

Based on my years in the classroom and reading about scientific findings, I always thought that historical discoveries created hard facts, but the archaeologists I met at this dig used phrases like:

"We don't really know."

"We haven't found evidence of..."

"We think..."

"We're questioning..."

"Maybe..."

I found their ability to not know interesting, because it goes with the adage: the older I get, the less I know. The more they know, they more they admit they aren't sure.

Am I the only one that finds this reassuring?

One younger archaeologist, in her early thirties with dirt smeared across her forehead, showed me her findings: human "poop" with some plant remains nearby.

She said, "We think that maybe they used plants for toilet paper."

She showed no discomfort in digging around ancient poop, rather her excitement was catching.

Ancient poop + plants (might) = ancient toilet paper.

The owner of the hotel drove me to another, more famous, ancient site that was only a few miles away, Çatalhöyük. This site has a larger team of full-time archaeologists that work up to eight hours a day. They use things like laser scanning and photo-modeling to create 3D images of what the mounds might have looked like long ago.

These mud houses were connected, thousands of houses at a time. The only way into the house was from a hole in the roof which kept the people safe from the wild animals roaming around outside. They think the only light in the houses was from the cooking/heating fire. When someone in the family died, they buried the dead under the floor. I'm guessing that even in death, their family members were protected from the wild animals.

The digs at this second site were larger, with huge domed tents built over the mounds. I went from never seeing an active archaeological dig to seeing two in one day.

My guide asked what we might do next. He knew I was going to

Cappadocia tonight, but I didn't need to catch a bus until the afternoon. He suggested we go and meet some nomads, and then have a picnic in the mountains.

I thought that sounded like a good idea. I wasn't sure what he meant by nomads, but figured it was another museum exhibit. I love museums.

After an hour of driving, we ended up on a dirt mountain road. There were no stores or houses in sight, we were in what appeared to be an abandoned area. I wondered where the museum was.

The countryside was beautiful: rolling hills, small trees, wildflowers. It was a dry area; I didn't see any water sources.

The owner of my hotel stopped the van on the side of the road. There was nothing around.

"We are here," he said.

I looked around, doubting that we were anywhere.

The two-year-old girl welcomed Holly Winter Huppert and her guide to her family's tent. Everything inside the tent was handwoven, including the tent.

The mother of the nomad family cooks over an open fire while her young daughter holds her from behind and her son looks on.

DAY 33B: KONYA: NOMADS

I got out of the van and looked around. Mountains. Valleys. Trees. Scrub brush. Where are we? I walked around to his side of the van.

My guide pointed to a random hill. "You okay to climb here or must we walk over there to where the hill is smaller?"

I said we could climb here and wanted to ask where we were going. Had I made a mistake spending the day with this man, a stranger?

The dirt was sandy; I had to climb quickly to get up the hill.

And there, next to a bank of trees, at the top of the hill there was a three-sided cloth tent set up on a flat area; sticks held up the roof.

Wait, when he said nomads, did he mean...?

He called out and a young woman appeared, who might have been in her late twenties. She smiled and greeted him by name. Her two-year-old daughter hid behind her. The mother wore colorful clothes with long sleeves and long pants, and she had a head scarf on. Her two-year-old daughter wore a long-sleeved shirt wrapped around her waist as a makeshift loincloth.

Wait...when he said nomads, did he mean...

We approached the tent and he showed me solar panels. "See?" he said. "They have everything they need."

Inside the tent on the right side, a washing machine was in the middle of a cycle, washing colorful clothes. The machine ran on solar power and was filled with buckets of water.

The young woman sat on the ground and cooked in a large frying pan over a small flame that was also on the ground. The tent was smaller than my bedroom at home and covered in a material that looked like burlap. The floors were covered in weavings. The only belongings I could see were mats that were probably sleeping mats, piled along the back edge of the tent and covered with more weavings.

We took off our shoes and sat on a mat on the ground.

So, when he said nomads, he meant people who live in tents and travel. I'd heard about them years ago and had a vague notion that they moved with the seasons and sold their animals to make money.

The shock of walking in on a life so different than mine was intense. I had a thousand questions but tucked them away. My job was to be present.

A family of five lived here, in this three-sided tent. There was no furniture, no bathrooms, no photographs on the walls, and no modern conveniences like a refrigerator or beds or rooms or even a door.

The mother quickly dressed her two-year-old daughter in clothes with long sleeves and long pants while she talked with a smile on her face for my guide, one of her husband's good friends. Her husband was away in town selling animals for the big holiday next week. The children told my guide that they were excited about the holiday.

He gave the family a large box of cookies and all four of them thanked him without taking their eyes from the package. He said it was for the holiday.

The two-year-old girl picked up a large, white onion. She watched us with wonder and started absentmindedly peeling the skin off the onion with her teeth, huge strips at a time. When she was satisfied that she had enough of the flesh showing, she took a big bite. Onion juice ran down her chin. She took another bite, then another.

The young woman's son, about 12 years old, entered and looked at me with big eyes. He sat on a pile of mats and listened as my guide and his mother talked. It goes without saying that there was no television or video games. I didn't see any books or toys or possessions of any kind.

The owner of my hotel teased the sister, who was around 10 years old, that he wanted to buy eggs, but she hadn't collected any yet. She smiled a big smile and left the tent with an old, plastic yogurt container.

The young girl picked up a knife, the size of a steak knife, and stabbed it into the same onion, then put the knife into her mouth to suck on the juices. I wasn't sure if this was a normal activity for her or if she was taking advantage of her mother's distraction.

The young woman saw her child with the knife and said something to the boy. He took the knife out of her mouth, but she was permitted to stick it into the onion again and again as she ate the chipped pieces that fell off.

The young woman continued cooking, and I worried we had interrupted their lunch.

The owner of the hotel boasted that the goat cheese this family makes is the best in Turkey. He said something in Turkish, and she brought me a sample of the cheese crumbles in a bowl with a spoon. I used my fingers to pick up a piece. Tangy. Sweet. A hint of salt? I said, "It's wonderful. Seriously. This is the best cheese," and smiled as big as I could so she might understand my pleasure.

The young woman smiled at me and motioned to the bowl, insisting I eat more.

I ate more.

Then she served tea. With sugar. The three children stared hard at the sugar container and I figured it must be a rare treat. Although I had not noticed my guide add sugar to his tea at breakfast and I never added sugar to my tea, we both accepted one small spoonful. I stirred the sugar into the tea, slowly.

When we had eaten our fill of cheese, the flies found the bowl. The two-year-old came over, waved the flies out of the way and used the spoon to eat more of the cheese. Her older brother scraped the bowl clean.

Nothing was wasted. Nothing.

My guide pointed to the weavings around the tent. "She wove all of this."

"These big floor mats. She wove them?"

"Yes. And the blankets. And the pillows. And the walls."

It was almost too much for my mind to understand. "She wove...the walls?"

"Yes. With goat hair."

Goat hair is woven into the walls; the oils on the hair repel water and keep the bugs out. The tent is waterproof.

I smiled at the young woman. I proudly told people around Turkey that my older sister is a weaver, an occupation that is highly regarded here.

Most people like to weave with wool from sheep, because the strands are long and it's easier to twist them into yarn. Goat's hair is short, it must be nearly impossible to weave.

I smiled at the young woman and nodded. I had so many questions.

A stick about three feet long hung from the ceiling and had yarn hanging down. This was her loom. She wove from the bottom to the top, then added more string to the top.

My guide boasted about something else and the older girl brought a round, plastic tub to me, opened it and put some dried herbs onto my hand.

"Thyme," my guide said. "They collect it from the hills, grind it and I help them sell it in town."

I wanted to buy some, but the US Customs laws do not permit spices into the US.

Too bad.

He paid the young woman for his previous order of cheese, as this cheese is the only cheese his family eats. He counted the money into her hand as the children watched.

The young woman insisted we stay for one more cup of tea, but we declined. We walked back to the van and the two-year-old followed us halfway down the hill and waved goodbye, again and again.

They don't get many visitors. I waved back, wishing I had something I could give her. A toy. A colorful piece of paper. A pen. But then I remembered that they had everything they needed.

Our van continued up the mountain road.

"I have many questions," I said.

"Ask me anything."

In the winter the family walks three days south to the Mediterranean area where it is warmer; they can get there so quickly because they know the shortcut. The young woman's husband drives the tractor with the tent and takes the two-year-old. He finds a location close to a school and sets up the next camp. The young woman and her children and the animals walk for three solid days to get to their next location.

The children go to school all year, then the family moves north again.

There was a problem where a random man was bullying them to pay money for camping there. He was a crook and somehow my guide helped them make the man stop the harassment, for which the woman expressed her gratitude, again.

If they suffer an emergency, they build a big fire outside and put evergreen branches into the flames. The big puff of smoke alerts others that they need help. People come. Nomads can call the ambulance, and it will come.

Her husband has a phone with internet on it. He is Facebook friends with his real-life friend, my guide. I had no idea of knowing how old her husband was, but my guide was close to 70 years old, so I didn't think they knew each other as children.

The children make their own toys from things they find in nature.

My guide said, "I lived this way until I was twelve. My family was nomads, too."

I thought my head might explode. He lived this way, too? "You lived in a tent with seven brothers and sisters?" I asked.

"Yes."

He said he loved living the nomad's life. The whole mountain was his playground.

I thought back to a conversation I had with his brother this morning during breakfast. He said that most people treat their houses like cages. They leave the cage to work or shop, then return to the cage the moment they are done. Rather than spend time in nature, they stay in their cages.

Now I understood his brother's opinions.

I asked my guide if he was teased at school for living outside, and he said that he wasn't invited to friends' houses because his clothes weren't very nice, but that everyone knew a nomad, so there was no teasing. He was accepted for who he was. He pointed out that about 30 percent of the students in his school lived a nomadic life. It wasn't rare.

The most dangerous part of being a nomad was the snakes. You had to watch out for them. He said that the snakes would find a nursing goat and suckle from her teat.

I said, doubting him, "You've seen a snake nurse from a goat?"

He looked right at me. "Of course. Yes. I have seen it. It is not common, but it happens."

I believed him.

I asked him if as a child he dreamed of living in a house.

"Yes."

When he was 12 years old, his primary school teacher talked to his father and said he needed to continue his education. So he and a cousin lived in a rented room in Konya, and had to fend for themselves for everything they needed.

The two of them learned to be completely independent by the age of 12. Clearly it was the right choice. He made it through school and high school and even attended university to become an English teacher, which was his career job.

At some point his grandfather tired of the nomadic life and they bought a house in a remote small town, close to where we were going to barbecue. We would ride through the town later.

We drove to the top of the mountain, which felt like we were on top of the world. There were vistas in all directions of sweeping valleys and small bushes and wind-battered trees.

The sun felt stronger and the wind blew harder and I felt like the luckiest woman alive for being on this tour. This was the way I liked to see a new place, far away from the crowds.

We stopped at the top of the mountain, unloaded the bags of meat and fruit and vegetables we bought in town, and carried them to a small pit my guide had used before.

"I want to show you how people cooked outside ten thousand years ago," he said.

He collected dry grasses and started a fire in the pit. He cut oak branches and stripped the leaves off and sharpened the ends. He pushed the meat and veggies onto the sticks and arranged them around the hot coals, then placed small rocks around the coals as a makeshift oven.

Two whole onions on one stick, two whole tomatoes on another stick. The peppers and meat got their own sticks, too.

As I continued asking questions, he moved the food around the makeshift oven so it would all finish cooking at the same time, an enviable skill for any outdoor cooking enthusiast.

He took a roasted tomato off the stick, cut it up for me and placed it on the same paper the raw meat had been wrapped in. We had no utensils or plates. A roasted pepper was placed on a rock next to me. So was a piece of roasted meat. I picked them up with my fingers and ate them happily.

You know how food always tastes better when you're camping? It tastes even better when you cook it outside on the top of a mountain with views that only the nomads have seen. I ate my fill, and he gave me more and more again.

"You will not eat dinner tonight because you will be on the bus," he said.

I accepted more food and said, "I may never need to eat again."

I continued to ask every question I could think of. He answered patiently and thoughtfully. I thanked him again and again. He said he wanted to show me other parts of Turkey, because I didn't have my "nose in the air" when I was visiting like many tourists do.

It was time to go, and he decided to drive through the small village where his family lived after being nomads, thinking that it would be a good place for me to see.

On the way to the village, he stopped to pick up two hitchhikers, an elderly couple carrying bags of produce from their plot of land that was miles from their house.

They climbed into the van with two giant bags filled with cucumbers, a jug of water, a bag of groceries and an old hoe. The man spoke in rapid Turkish to my guide, who translated for me.

"Several cars passed them by and wouldn't stop to pick them up.

Everyone knows them, and they can't believe anyone would refuse to help them."

The old man continued speaking fast.

"He says he wouldn't hurt anyone."

When we arrived at the town, the hitchhikers gifted my guide with a pile of cucumbers. I watched as the hitchhikers and the guide both expressed gratitude for the other. The guide acted as if the old people had done us a favor by riding with us.

We arrived at the village, where his father still has a house.

It was a small community of small houses, set on a hill; most houses had only a few small rooms. Most of the young people leave the town for jobs in the larger cities. We sat with the guide's friends, a father and a son, and ate grapes from their vines.

The 30-something-year-old son told a story of meeting a woman who accepted his proposal to marry, which was a big deal in this small town.

We wished him well and accepted more grapes for our ride back to Konya.

As we rode to the bus station that was over an hour away, my guide said there was something very important he wanted to tell me.

I looked at him.

He said, "You have a wild side about you. A normal life will never satisfy you."

I didn't expect him to talk about me in such a familiar way, but I listened to his words. A normal life will never satisfy me.

Was it more surprising that he could see this about me, or that I didn't know this about myself? I spend so much energy trying to fit into my surroundings. Perhaps there was wisdom in his words.

He continued, "You must work to nurture this wild side of you, or you will never be happy."

I mumbled something about appreciating his ideas, and I did appreciate them, but I tucked his suggestion away for a different time.

I must nurture my wild side.

Got it.

The young girl eats a raw onion as a snack.

The guide pays for the cheese while the children watch.

The guide wanted to show how the nomads cooked ten thousand years ago. It is the way his family cooked when he was a child; his family was nomadic when he was young.

Holly Winter Huppert with the guide (and now a friend) Mehmet at the bus station.

The man who serves the complimentary drinks on the bus watches out the front window as the bus approaches the closed bus station.

A view of Cappadocia

DAY 33C: KONYA: BUS

At the bus station my guide helped me find the ticket booth and told them where I was going. I needed to take a bus to a town, then take a smaller bus to my smaller town, then walk to my hotel.

Great. No problem.

My guide talked to my bus driver for a long time, telling him where I needed to go. After so many bus rides where I guessed my way along, I was glad for the extra help.

I sat in my designated seat, #14. A young woman, maybe 20 years old, with long sleeves and long pants and a head scarf, sat in the next seat looking out the window. After I sat down, she called to the young man who serves drinks and asked him something in a quiet voice.

It was okay. I was sure she was asking for me to move; I didn't mind. I was willing to sit anywhere.

The young man who served the drinks left and came back with a water for the young woman. She said something else to the man and he left again.

I wondered where I would sit next.

The man handed her another water and she handed a water to me with a big smile.

My surprise made her laugh. I bowed my head and thanked her. She nodded quickly.

On the other side of the aisle, a man sat with his mother. He asked me where I was from, in English.

I braced myself, ready for his upset. "America," I said. "New York."

He said, "I have never been there, but I hear it is very nice."

The sister I stayed with in Atabey sent me a message after my last bus ride and suggested I never get on a bus that is going to the eastern part of the country, as the people who live there can be unfriendly to travelers. She was right; my last bus was heading east and had many people who didn't want to sit next to me. The east is notorious for being closed-minded to tourists.

This bus was heading north.

The man who served the drinks picked up my empty water container and motioned to me, asking if I wanted another.

I didn't, but appreciated being asked.

The bus stopped in a center, and the man sitting next to me told me in English that there was a 30-minute break time.

I made my way to the restroom and when I went back into the restaurant, the man and his mother insisted I sit with them.

Wow. What a difference a bus ride makes.

The man told me not to worry, even if the driver forgot or the boy who serves water forgot, he would help me find my bus stop.

I thanked him and when I got back on the bus, I noticed the young woman who sat next to me wasn't there yet.

I mentioned it to the man across the aisle, who alerted the staff. After talking, the man who served the water ran into the center.

The man sitting across the aisle said, "She is probably praying."

A few minutes later, the man and the woman climbed back onto the bus. She held her hands over her face and apologized to everyone she passed. The driver smiled at her and so did the others on the bus. No hard feelings.

I couldn't imagine people in New York being so forgiving to a stranger who delayed a bus's departure.

She sat in her seat and pantomimed to me that she had been praying and lost track of time. She placed her hand over her heart, then moved it up and down fast, miming that her heart was racing. She turned to the window to finish her prayers.

So the rest-stop centers were included in the bus's schedule as a time to eat food, smoke a cigarette, use the bathroom and pray.

Got it.

I napped some more.

It was after nine o'clock when my bus made it to my station. There were no minibuses there and no taxi cabs. The station was closed.

I thought this could be an interesting transition but wasn't worried. I could get someone to call a taxi for me. People here were so kind.

The man who serves drinks had me get off the bus and stand under a ledge out of the pouring rain. Then he ran from bus to bus to gather information. He went back to the driver and made a report; I was waved back on the bus.

The man sitting across the aisle was as surprised as I was.

The bus drove into the night. The man who serves the drinks told the man across the aisle from me that they were driving me into the city center so I could get a bus.

Wait, so the whole bus is being hijacked for my poor planning? I played away my day and came too late; now the bus was going out of its way to help me out?

Wow.

My general rule was to show up in my new town by 3:00 PM so I had time to find my way before it got dark. I was many hours behind this schedule.

After ten minutes of driving, I wondered how long until I arrived at my next decision. That's what traveling is to me, one decision after another. Twenty minutes into the extended drive and I wondered if the bus driver had made my next decision for me.

Twenty-five minutes later, the man sitting across the aisle went up to the driver and asked him something. He returned to me and said, "The driver said he didn't forget you."

Over a half hour after the extended bus drive, the bus pulled over. I once again said goodbye to the man, his mother and the girl sitting next to me. I got to the door of the bus and the man who serves the drinks told me to sit down.

Seriously?

After a few more minutes I was called off the bus. The boy who serves the drinks was standing in the rain next to the bus driver. It was a dark, rainy night. "Luggage?"

I showed them which suitcase was mine. The bus driver lifted it out of the compartment and pulled it down the sidewalk himself. It is highly unusual for a bus driver to help with luggage. In the rain. In the night. When he had a schedule to keep and many, many more hours to drive in the opposite direction.

Two men stood at the end of the block, in the rain, in the dark. We walked towards them.

I could hear the voice of my uncle Rudy, who passed away several years ago. He was an avid traveler. "This is getting more interesting by the minute, eh?" I heard his long laugh.

If one of the two men standing there was the Grim Reaper, I wouldn't have been surprised. Who else would be standing out in the rain late at night?

One of the men spoke. "We are taxi drivers. If you tell us where you are going, we will take you there."

I smiled big relief and thanked them.

The bus driver stood next to me, staring at the taxi drivers.

I smiled and thanked the bus driver, relieving him of his duties.

The bus driver stood his ground.

The taxi driver explained, "The driver will not leave you unless you are comfortable that we are the right taxi drivers for you."

I nodded my head in an enthusiastic "Yes" and the driver shook my hand. I shook the hand of the man who served the drinks and mouthed a silent "thank you" to the people on the bus, who didn't complain about being dragged over an hour off schedule.

Today I studied an ancient civilization that gave up its nomadic ways, met people who live a nomadic life, ate a typical nomadic lunch cooked by a former nomad and traveled to my next destination, dragging my belongings behind me; a bit of a nomad myself.

Turkey was taking very, very good care of me.

DAY 34: GÖREME: MARS

I stopped and stared; nothing prepares you for seeing your first giant fairy chimneys of Cappadocia. (See photo on the previous page.) These are leftover volcanic rock formations that have been withered by weather and then carved into caves that are big enough to live in, have restaurants inside, and some have been made into hotels.

Imagine a rock formation large enough to live in.

They're striking to look at; some people liken them to the surface of Mars.

I walked off the main road in town and walked to the valley. People rode horses or ATVs out into the valley; I hiked with other adventurers. I was dusty and dry, but the views of these rock formations kept the explorer in me curious. One more kilometer. What's down that path?

I met a man from Spain who said his favorite thing he did in town was attend a "Turkish Night" show in a neighboring town. Really? Years ago I went to a tourist show in Mexico and it was fantastic, with costumes and dances from around the country, and the entrance fee included a spectacular dinner. Maybe the Turkish Night would be as good?

I found a travel agent and bought a ticket that included a driver to and from the show and dinner for less than $20. Why not?

The hotel room I chose in Göreme was not the kind of room I wanted to leave. It was beautifully furnished, had decorative lamps, fancy shades, a comfortable bed and a huge bathroom. Though the name of the hotel had the word "cave" in it, it was a mock cave: the ceiling was curved to give it a cave-look.

Fake cave? It sounds horrible but it was a total delight. All the modern conveniences, including a stellar view out the window and hand-carved furniture.

The only problem with a comfortable bed is getting out of it in the morning. I climbed up onto the roof at sunrise to catch the hot air balloons taking off. They sounded like a hundred Darth Vaders floating by, colorful, floating, and peaceful yet gasping for air.

Napping became my second activity of the day, and then my third activity. I ran out of water, so I had to force myself, again, to get up and shower and dress, and was about to go out to find some more water when the maid knocked on my door and brought me two fresh bottles.

How did she know?

No, really. How did she know?

I celebrated by drinking one bottle, then climbing back into bed for one more nap. Traveling can be exhausting. When people asked me later in town what I like about the Göreme area, I said the cooler weather made it great for napping, and the fairy chimneys were unlike anything I've ever seen before.

Since I'd napped away my morning, I hiked through the valley for a few hours and then bought my ticket for some late-night culture. The travel agency apologized that my driver wouldn't speak English, as if it's an unwritten rule that all locals must speak the language of every visiting country.

"Merhaba," I said to my driver.

He returned the hello. A few minutes later I said again, "Merhaba" and he laughed, understanding that it was the only word that I could say in a social situation.

The center that held the Turkish Night performance was a giant concrete building, fashioned to look like...a cave. Yes, that was planned.

The meal started with a nice selection of meze, my favorite appetizers, including yogurt: I love a cuisine that includes yogurt with every meal.

The yogurt in Turkey has been notable. So far, my only regret of the trip stemmed from the hotel in Konya offering me another breakfast serving of the best yogurt I'd ever eaten, ever, and I declined. I was full and chose that very moment to cut down on my yogurt obsession.

Why?

So it was no surprise that I started this meal with yogurt. Likely it was a full-fat yogurt spiced with garlic and a touch of pepper, an amazing combination.

I dug my spoon in for the first taste. No good. Really not good. It was sour.

Wait. Really? Spoiled yogurt?

I waited a moment and tried it again, just in case that first bite wasn't representative of the whole dish. I know, that whole quote about doing the same thing and expecting a different outcome, but yogurt is my favorite food group: I was giving it another chance.

If there was a word, sour-er, this yogurt would be that. I tried to alert the staff, so they might avoid a catastrophic wave of unhappy customers who complain about being served old food, but their English wasn't good enough, so they simply removed the spoiled yogurt from my table.

But wait. If the yogurt was sour, how was the food?

I had walked past the kitchen on my way into the center. A chef in a clean white apron stood next to an empty stainless-steel table. Where was the food? Shouldn't he be busy chopping and cutting and filling trays to feed the two hundred people who were here to eat?

I dated a chef years ago who said to never trust a chef with a clean apron. Noted.

Old food. I lost my appetite and nibbled some cheese and pickled vegetables. Later I accepted a lamb dinner. Wait, did they boil the lamb?

The staff was not concerned that I didn't eat much, but they worried that I didn't want any alcohol and kept bringing me better and more expensive selections. I tried to tell them that I don't drink, but that made them even more resolute to find some kind of spirits for me to enjoy. Alcohol was included in the price.

I know. I know. But I stopped drinking years ago when I tired of hangovers.

When the show started, it became clear that it would have been more enjoyable if I were filled with alcohol like the many multi-aged Americans in attendance who were traveling in large buses. I think the yogurt might have passed the mustard, too, if I'd been drinking.

There were some interesting dances and traditional costumes. The men danced alone. The women danced alone. They danced together. For the most part, the audience treated the show as a prerecorded event: They talked loudly and took selfies with their friends and waited for what they considered the main attraction: an invitation for them to join the dancers on the stage.

The belly dancer was quite good, I'd been wanting to see a belly dance show in Turkey, but this was the first one I'd found so far; likely there would be more in Istanbul. This dancer had all the moves from swivels to hair flipping, and she did get the attention of the crowd with her beautiful red dress.

She started teaching the drunken Americans how to dance, but her charges would break into silly side dances—to make each other laugh —rather than following her lead. Most of the paying crowd wanted to do their own thing.

To appease the drunks, the center played the song, "YMCA" in English so the tourists could take over the dance floor. They did. They danced, they shouted. They moved their arms to match the letters in the song.

I was overcome with embarrassment that my culture couldn't escape itself. It's as if our very identity is held in who we have always been and nothing can open that door, not a belly dancer with a sparkly costume or dancers dressed in traditional costumes.

It was the first time on my trip that I spent time under the same roof with people from the United States who were only looking for a good photo opportunity, not a cultural experience. In hanging with my people, I felt out of place. How could we be so different?

On the way to the center tonight, my driver's friend rode along with us. She asked me pointed questions about what I liked about Turkey.

I told her I liked many things. Cucumbers and cheese for breakfast. Yogurt with every meal. Diversity in dress. Many free museums. A kindness in people who are always available to help me or stray cats or a beggar on the street. Clean streets. Many musical styles. Ancient ruins. The sea. The cities on the sea. Carpets. Pottery. The freshest food.

She interrupted me and said, "You have been paying attention. This is unusual."

If only I could leave early. I'd seen enough.

My driver arrived early to check on me. "Merhaba!" I said, as I gathered my things and pointed towards the exit so he would know I was ready to go.

As we walked out, a woman we walked past asked her friend in English, "Where do you think she's going? Another party?"

Yeah, another party. A party of one.

Waiting to get in to see the next cave at the Göreme Outdoor Museum.

Sunrise from the roof of Holly Winter Huppert's hotel in Cappadocia.

DAY 35: GÖREME: SHUFFLE

"No stop. Fast only. Walk," the Turkish guard shouted at me and the other tourists that were crammed into a small cave dwelling, once used as a church in the Göreme Outdoor Museum.

Frescos lined the walls. I had never seen beautiful art painted in a cave.

"Move more. No stop," he demanded.

He was ruining the experience. I tuned him out.

This art. Every wall was covered. Faded reds and oranges. Church elders? Religious signs and crosses. There was something beautiful about viewing art that was primitively painted on walls.

I'd read about how after the paintings were discovered, people were encouraged to throw rocks at the art, trying to scratch the paintings off the walls. Muslims don't believe in adding human forms—especially faces—in artwork, preferring symbols for their religious art. So when a new ruler came to town, the religion changed, the locals were encouraged to deface the art.

It's a marvel that any paint is left on the walls at all. I was so busy studying the art, that I forgot the "No photo!" rule and reached for my camera.

I framed the fresco on the back of my digital camera and snapped.

"You. America," the guard screamed from several feet away. "No camera. No photo."

I turned to see who he was shouting at. Me? He was shouting at me?

My camera was in my hand. Oh, right. I just took a photo. Would he believe me if I told him I took the photo subconsciously? That recording the things I see had become so automatic that I wasn't aware that I was doing it?

Luckily there were many people between us, I think he would have stomped my camera if he were closer to me.

I returned my camera to the special pocket in my purse and zipped the purse shut, glad to have an extra barrier between me and my subconscious. It was either that or tie my arm behind my back.

The guard glared at me. I worried for a moment that he would demand I erase the entire photo card, which happened once when I was taking photos on an Indian reservation in Arizona where I taught kindergarten many years ago. In the end the Native Police showed up, lights flashing, and went against my Native American accuser and let me keep those photographs.

But this Turkish guard was correct; the signs were clearly posted at the entrance to every cave. How do you explain in Turkish that the photo took itself?

The guard pointed his glare at someone else and I shuffled out of that cave and lined up for the next one, a rare souvenir saved on my camera.

Score!

I had hiked up the hill to the outdoor museum yesterday, and the crowds were of such high numbers that the guy at the ticket booth suggested that I return this morning at 8:30. He promised that the crowds wouldn't get big until 10:00.

He was wrong. It was 9:00, and I watched as bus after bus dropped off more people who wanted to see the caves that had been turned into churches and then decorated.

I had to wait in line to get into a cave, then shuffle through a slow-moving line to look at what there was to see. This wasn't the tourist experience I was looking for, but I made myself continue the Cave Shuffle.

I had gone to the underground city next to Nevşehir yesterday, an hour before closing. There was a time when up to twenty thousand people (!) lived below ground while they waited for conquering armies to tire of looking for them. They lived down there with their livestock and their food storage. In the dark. With air piped in from above. For years.

Years.

For a fee, visitors can climb through the underground city that has many different levels. I really wanted to see it.

A guide I met in town recommended I arrive an hour before closing, because the lines would be shorter. I timed my arrival perfectly, but the lines snaked around all available spaces. They sent me away at the ticket booth; I wouldn't make it inside before it closed.

Today was my last full day in the valley, so I would miss visiting the underground cities. If I wanted to see the church frescos, this was my only opportunity.

I almost skipped the Dark Church, the biggest and most impressive church in the bunch. There was a 45-minute wait. It was hot outside. And dry. And I was tired of watching people taking selfies as if the rest of us were a backdrop to their lives. I was tired of shuffling, or even worse, I was tired of standing still.

It's not like I had something else to do, I could wait. I shifted my attention to the shoes tourists wore. A lot of sneakers. A lot of flat sandals. Several women, who may have been on their honeymoon, wore heels. I watched them scurrying up hills and over crumbling steps as their men rushed them along.

Oh, you poor, poor women.

If we checked in with these same women in ten years, would they complain that their marriages were...uncomfortable? Would they wonder how that happened? Would they understand that for years they lied to their husbands, insisting that heels are as comfortable as flats? I'm all for fashion, but not at ancient ruins.

Me? I packed three pairs of shoes, as the travel experts suggest you trade between different shoes every day for the comfort of your feet. I bought a pair of flat Clark sandals just before I left, and they were so darn comfortable that I wore them every day, with the rare trade to a different pair of shoes.

When it comes to advice about shoes, I listen to my feet.

It cost extra to get into the Dark Church, but my museum card covered it. Only twenty people could enter at a time. The guard who sat at the front of the small space welcomed us with a quiet voice and told us to take our time, enjoy the paintings but take no photographs.

There was a sensation of feeling in this space; I relaxed and let the art enter my body. Though it was a small space, it was as if I were getting a hug just by standing there. A colorful art hug.

After the muted frescos in the other churches, the restored frescos in the Dark Church boasted vibrant colors and an intensity that put me into a state of awe.

This. This was amazing. One painting next to another painting. The size of the painting matched the space. People. Animals. Signs. Every bit of wall was painted.

The beauty of this church makes all other churches in the world seem cold and plain with their white walls.

Just to be showy, the carvers of this church added columns for decorative purposes. I walked around four or five times, then crawled through the basement in case there were more paintings downstairs. There weren't.

I left this cave knowing my trip up the mountain had been worth it.

Wait. Something was different. Outside. What was different?

When I went into the church, there were so many people you couldn't walk at a normal pace. Now there were so few people you could jog to the next church if you wanted to. The crowds were gone. Gone.

I worried that there'd been some kind of national security crisis, or something. There were less than ten other people wandering around, which meant I was practically alone. If something were wrong, they would tell us, right?

I went to the next cave church, no lines at all. I walked around while the guide played on his phone. There was only one fresco, a muted one.

Who could I ask about the sudden change in population?

I looked at my watch as if it might have the answer. It was 12:00. Wow, I'd been at the museum for four hours already.

Oh, that's where the people went. Lunchtime. They left to find food.

I was glad to see them go. Me? I was far from hungry.

When traveling, you must adjust to the circumstances around you, be it a lack of empathy or excessive crowds or intolerable heat or sudden elbow room.

And so I discarded my Cave Shuffle and walked to the next cave.

It was another good one.

Inside the Hagia Sophia in Istanbul.

The narrow stairs at the Terrace Guest House in Istanbul.

DAY 36: ISTANBUL: CHOICES

I followed the nephew of the owner of the hotel up a winding staircase, grateful he was carrying my suitcase. These were the thinnest steps I had ever seen inside a building, only the ball of my foot fit on the widest part of the step.

There was one hotel room at the first landing, #3. One room for the whole floor?

We climbed another set of thin, winding steps. On the second-floor landing there was one hotel room: #4. Really? One room? Are they enormous rooms?

It reminded me of the children's book, *Sideways Stories from Wayside School* where the school has one classroom per floor, so students must climb ridiculous amounts of stairs to get to class. That book always makes kids laugh.

And now my hotel is mimicking a children's book. It's a good thing I'm not being shown room #412, because it might be up 412 flights of stairs.

Actually there are only eight rooms in this hotel. Small. Homey. Family run.

The nephew gave me the choice between two rooms, #7 or #8. I like choices.

On the third-floor landing, without any explanation as to what happened to room #5, we happened upon rooms #6 and #7. He fiddled with the key to #7 and we walked in. View. There's a water view. Look at that view. Rooftops. Restaurants with rooftop decks. People walking around on the sidewalks below. And the jewel of the view, the Golden Horn waterway, right there, dividing old Istanbul and the newer section.

I was standing in Europe; I could see Asia.

The room was small, the bathroom small. But that view!

We climbed more stairs to get a look at #8, the only room on the top floor that sat next to the breakfast room. He opened the door to a large room with double beds and large windows. The views here were of the Blue Mosque and Hagia Sophia, beautiful views.

One of the reasons I chose this hotel was that it had better views than the opulent Four Seasons Hotel that was next door. In fact, the people who pay roughly five times the price that I paid had a great view of the back of my hotel. Sure, their rooms are probably ten times the size, and I bet they get robes and slippers and soft music playing in the lobby, but, hey... I got the view.

Room #8 was larger, but there was no water view from inside the room. I wanted the water view.

This was my twelfth and final room in Turkey. My hotel room is the gateway to the city I am visiting, so finding a safe and comfortable place takes hours of research for each stop on my journey. I look at websites and read reviews and read the one guidebook I carried with me on the trip.

It's difficult to figure out what part of town I want to stay in when considering a foreign city. Sometimes I research to find out what part of the city the Hilton Hotel is in; it's often in the better parts of town.

In Izmir the Hilton was only $50 a night at the time I was there. I had no interest in staying in an American hotel, but knew that if I needed an oasis of safety during the trip, I could find my way there. I chose the Piano Hotel, which was about a six-minute walk from the Hilton, and was completely happy with my choice.

For my Konya stay, I did a lot of research, knowing that I would go see the whirling dervishes at night, and really wanted an interesting place that was close enough to walk back to the hotel. I found that place.

When trying to decide if I should visit Istanbul, I met two Turkish women on the ferry to Greece who suggested that I stay close to the Blue Mosque and Hagia Sophia, because that way I could spend my days touring the city, and if I got lost everyone could direct me back to the Blue Mosque.

That was great advice.

I'll list all of my hotels thus far so I might remember them in the future. And a note for anyone who adds up the cost of these rooms and thinks I must be related to the Queen of England: we got a raise at work that was retroactive for two years. Hello. That money paid for these rooms, and my tax refund paid for the plane ticket.

I'd been super careful with money while traveling, but likely would be eating beans and rice for a few weeks after I returned home until I earned another paycheck. No complaints; so worth it!

～

Izmir (The Piano Hotel)

Loved this place. $35 a night. I stayed in Room 301. Small, but a great setup. The breakfast was one of the best I'd seen in Turkey, a buffet in a room with a street view and the constant tink-tink-tink of people stirring sugar into their tea glass. The staff is very kind and helpful. The location was perfect. Would stay again.

～

Çeşme/Çiftlik (Çiftlik Butik Otel)

Beautiful location. $45 a night. I had a pool/garden view. Great sunsets. Breakfast is served: beautiful selection. Staff kind and helpful. Walk to Çiftlik which is a small, friendly town with a hint of beach. There is a bus to Çeşme. Would not stay again, too far away and the Çeşme crowd of yachters and uber-expensive shops are not my crowd.

～

Selçuk/Ephesus (Stayed with a super cool family)

Love this town. Small, walkable. Friendly. Close to Ephesus, Mother Mary's House and the beach. Great Saturday market. Amazing food and the best lemonade I've ever had, at Queen Bee restaurant. Love the family I stayed with, will visit again because they have become family. Really, I will return. #familynow #willreturn

∽

Denizli/Pamukkale (Yildirim Hotel)

Right across from the bus station. $15 a night. Wish I remembered my room number. I had a balcony and a view of the bus station—I was that close. Breakfast buffet, good selection, nothing too exciting. Staff kind and helpful. Denizli has an okay bazaar and an interesting old cemetery. Easy to get a bus to Pamukkale from here. There was a riot/demonstration when I visited. Would stay again but might prefer to stay at Pamukkale to get extra time there.

∽

Atabey (Stayed with super cool sisters and their family)

Stayed with two sisters. One of my funniest memories of my trip is when the sisters and I were in the kitchen preparing breakfast and all three of us had a hot flash in the same moment. #rare #funny. Loved this small town and the area around it but would only visit again to hang with this sweet family. I love these women and will see them again. #friends #forever.

∽

Antalya (Minyon Hotel)

$85 a night. Great location, in the tourist bubble. Beautiful garden with a motorized awning that shades you from the sun. #hightec The owner is on the premises helping. Great location. Breakfast costs extra. Great room and bathroom. Interesting town. I loved the hamam just down the street. Would stay in the area again but prefer to be outside the tourist bubble.

∿

Çıralı/Olympos (Uğur Pansiyon)

$40 a night for a cabin across the street from a rocky beach. Great sunrises. Not a practical place to stay without a car, 20-minute walk to town, 40-minute walk to the ruins of Olympos. Few streetlights at night to walk back from town. The air conditioner didn't work well and was in the living room, not the bedroom. Cute town, "unspoiled" and my Turkish friends love the area. Very family-oriented place: the families kept to themselves. Breakfast buffet quite good, included in price. Owners on-site, very helpful. Would not stay again but would consider something closer to town on another visit.

∿

Kaş/Greece (Pinar Pension)

I had one night here before I could get to my next place. Smallest room ever, by design: I wanted to be in town, and it was the only room available, sadly it was only available for one night. Smallest bathroom ever. Best rooftop deck with views of the sea. Breakfast buffet good, included in price. Walkable: great location, love Kaş. Super friendly/helpful staff continued to help after I left since the next place wasn't friendly. Would stay again.

∿

Kaş, center (****)

$70 a night. Least favorite room on the trip. How did this place get good reviews? My room was a cell with bare walls that had cracks in them. A small window gave the only natural light. Electricity cuts out. Air conditioner broken: wouldn't/couldn't turn off. Noisy roosters in the back garden crowing twenty-four hours a day. Owner on-site, not friendly or helpful. Breakfast included but served late. Walkable. Great town. Great restaurant next door, Bi Lokma. (Get their Meze Plate.)

(They made a mistake and Expedia didn't charge me for the room and though I checked in with her twice, the owner didn't figure out that I hadn't paid until after I left. I spent hours trying to sort it out on the road and after I returned home, without the owner's help: she said she was too busy to deal with it. The owner demands that I give her my credit card number. Um. No. Twice she sent me her banking information, both times her numbers were wrong. How is she still in business? Finally paid through Western Union, and she complained that she wanted to charge interest for the late fee. Would not recommend ever, ever, ever.)

～

Konya/Rumi (Konya Dervish Hotel)

$50 a night. Owned and run by two brothers, both on-site helping and both speak English. They also have a carpet shop on-site; I didn't buy anything. Beautiful room decorated with antiques and three antique carpets, hello! It's like you're visiting someone's home. Amazing breakfast included in price. Walkable. The Rumi museum is nearby, so is the cultural center where the dervishes dance on Saturday nights starting at 7:00. One brother, Mehmet, and I hung out for a most memorable tour that was tailored to fit my interests. I will return one day and stay longer.

～

Cappadocia/Göreme (Lucky Cave Hotel)

$50 a night. Room #106. Looks drab from outside but inside is the most beautiful place with beautiful gardens, a glass-enclosed breakfast room, and a room beautifully decorated with hand-carved furniture. Room large, bathroom large. Amazing breakfast, included. Great rooftop deck for viewing the morning's hot air balloons. Manager on-site is very helpful. The 24-hour reception desk is unusual for Turkey. Walkable to Göreme Outdoor Museum. Great hiking trails by foot or rent four-wheelers or horses. If I return to the area, I will stay here again.

~

Istanbul (Terrace Guest House)

$100 a night. Amazing location in the Old Town, close to the Blue Mosque and the Hagia Sophia. Excellent water views from my room, #7. Small room. Small balcony. Family run. Quiet. Owner helpful about what to do in the city—steered me towards the best ice cream, the best places for dinner and gave me a free pass for the tram. Breakfast room and rooftop deck with amazing views. Great breakfast, included. Also sells carpets on-site. I will return.

~

Room #7 won my favor. I stood on the balcony staring at the views and might have stood there all night, but wanted to check out the neighborhood. I wandered along the walking street that offered great people-watching, with fashionable people coming and going, some on vacation, some heading to a night out. Vendors in the square sold roasted corn and roasted chestnuts.

I wanted to buy some cut-up fruit from a vendor, but there was nobody inside the booth. A man walked up to me and said the cost of the honeydew melon was 12 lira.

Wait. Did this man even work here?

I stood looking at him, wondering if he were a street bum and if I would get arrested for eating fruit that I didn't pay the real vendor for.

I asked if he worked here.

"Yes," he said. "Pay now, fast. For you ten lira."

Why did I have to pay him fast? It was dark out; I have this rule that I never go out at night by myself. I'd gone against this safety measure because I'd just arrived and wanted to see the neighborhood.

The man took a puff on his cigarette said, "Okay. For you eight lira."

Wow. This was the best bargaining tip ever. Say nothing, just stand and stare.

I shrugged.

He reached inside the booth and grabbed a fork and a napkin.

Maybe he did work here. I handed him the money and walked away while eating chunks of sweet melon.

I'd chosen well.

A communal cup at a water fountain in Istanbul.

A busy marketplace in Istanbul.

DAY 37: ISTANBUL: SAFE

My friend Amy texted to let me know that there was a major earthquake in the western part of Turkey yesterday. I didn't feel anything here but reached out to friends who live in the earthquake zone, and they are safe.

This reminded me that I need to keep my devices charged so I would be prepared if there were a power outage.

I returned to my room and charged my phone, my tablet and my back-up battery.

On my way out for an early dinner, I walked past the Blue Mosque, a building more majestic than, and unlike, any building I've seen before, and thought again about how fortunate I was to stay in this part of town so I could venture past the site several times every day.

A man who might have been 35 years old stood off to the side and called to me with great excitement, as if he couldn't believe he'd found me:

"Australia?"

I ignored him and kept walking.

He dropped his voice to a regular tone. "You from Australia?"

I turned my head away from him and walked on.

He walked next to me, and whined, "Why you no talk me?"

I considered the themes the scammers use to build trust. This one used recognition, familiarity and hurt feelings. Did they take classes in how to manipulate strangers?

I walked into a store; he didn't follow me. I browsed the cheap souvenirs that had nothing to do with Turkey. Colorful bookmarks. Small wooden spoons. Postcards of kittens. A worker stood in front of me and held up a coordinated set of Turkish towels. How do you say, "I'm just here for the air conditioning?"

I returned to the sidewalk and continued my walk. That man was gone, but there was another just a block away.

This one was cuter with longer hair. It's as if there was a consortium trying to figure out which scammer I would fall for. Woman alone, send in a man. Older. Younger. Holding a book. Longer hair.

"Where you from?" Longer-hair asked.

I ignored him.

"Holland!"

I exhaled slowly. I've figured out that there are more manipulators in the park between the Hagia Sophia and the Blue Mosque, but they are everywhere.

Sometimes they perch at tourist sites and offer their assistance on finding an entrance or explaining the rules, then suggest a cup of tea and charge a large fee for their help.

"I don't like tea," I'd said almost every day, without offering eye contact.

"Carpets? You like carpets? We look carpets."

"Nope." I'd walk on. "I don't like carpets."

"Can I see passport? I love passport."

I smile and say as fast as I can, so there is no chance that he can translate, "Could I borrow five thousand dollars? There's a horse..."

I know, it's their job, to befriend a foreigner and steal her money and passport. I get it, foreign passports are worth a mint on the black market. These scammers have families they need to support, quotas they need to fill, but I'm not an easy target.

In Ecuador years ago, someone squirted ketchup on me and offered a napkin to clean it up. I held my purse tighter and told them I love ketchup art and refused to let them clean it. It's a scam to distract and rob.

Once when traveling in Mexico, someone tapped my right shoulder and I quickly turned to the left; there was a grandmother with her hand in position, waiting for me to turn the other way. "Noooooooo," I shouted, as if I were reprimanding a child who was about to cross a busy street without looking both ways, and the grandmother and the shoulder-tapper both ran off.

Yesterday I met two women who were college students from Ireland. They told me a sad story about letting a man buy them drinks in Istanbul. They said it was a fun night, until they both realized their passports were missing.

"I wore my purse on my body the whole night," the woman wearing the miniskirt said.

"Me too," her friend wearing a plunging neckline added.

I held back my mommy-voice and didn't remind them about how lucky they were that their only problem was a lack of paperwork.

We were standing in a mob of people waiting for a tram. As the women told me their story, a Turkish man approached them and said, "I buy you drink. Now. Come me."

The girls looked at each other and talked back and forth, deciding. I thought they were going to decline, for obvious reasons, but they didn't.

"We could use a drink!" they both said.

My mommy-voice could hide no longer. I said, "He wants your new passport."

The man agreed with me. He actually agreed with me.

"Yes. I like passport. Can I look you?"

They both started rummaging through their purses. Seriously? Had they learned nothing?

I turned to the man. "Go away."

He ignored me.

"Girls," I said.

They looked up.

"He's going to steal your passports. Do you think Ireland will be happy to get you updated papers, again?"

That stopped them.

"Passport?" the man said, as if he were a customs agent.

The girls stopped rummaging and told him to leave.

I left too. It's dangerous to spend time with slow learners.

This man with the long hair tried to win my trust as I passed by the Blue Mosque on my way to dinner. "I buy you drink, now."

"No, thank you."

"Tea. We drink tea."

Tourists are warned to never turn down an invitation to tea, but I could not drink that much caffeine in a day, so I turned down tea offers all day long. "No, thank you."

"You need drugs?"

"No, thank you."

"You have passport?"

I declined every question until he tired and left me. I knew the way to the restaurant and took a longer route so I could enjoy some people-watching.

I noticed the patterns of women's shirts: small prints, large American words that meant nothing (Give me a break), (Doors for Sale or Rent), and my favorite (Rot with Me!). There were also crop tops with glitter words in English (I'm a Rainbow), blouses with lines and tank tops with stripes.

I wondered if "Rot with Me" was a synonym for "Grow Old with Me," or if it were closer to "Rot in Hell"?

Then there was an entire style set for conservative women who covered their heads and wore long sleeves and long pants that were solid, flowered, sparkled or plain black cloth.

I had walked past a store selling underwear earlier in the day, and was surprised to see a group of women who were fully covered standing in front of scantily clad mannequins wearing G-strings. I figured that they were making fun of the lack of modesty, but then the women entered the store.

I had so much to learn.

My choice for dinner tonight was a restaurant called Matbah in the old part of Istanbul that boasted a menu dedicated to the same foods the sultans ate during the Ottoman Empire. (A king rules the whole kingdom, a sultan rules a part of that kingdom.)

I ordered the quail baked in eggplant that was drizzled with a pomegranate and pepper paste sauce. Delicate. Sweet. Spicy.

My waiter used tongs to place a roll on my plate.

I flinched, as if it were a poisonous spider. "No. No bread," I said. "No gluten. No bread." I took out my dietary requirements, written in Turkish, that he'd already read that explained my celiac disease and my need to eat a specialized diet. I handed the paper to him, again.

The waiter pointed to the roll. "No bread."

"No bread," I repeated. "No gluten." I should have stuck with my boring lamb shish. I could have gotten some extra yogurt on the side, as I did most nights. I wanted something different, but I didn't want to get sick. Setting gluten next to the food I would eat could make me sick, and cranky.

He handed me an empty plastic wrapper with words printed on the side. I recognized the word that was probably gluten. I looked at the waiter.

He pointed to the roll. "No gluten."

That poisonous spider turned into a dove before my eyes. "Gluten-free bread?"

The waiters surrounded me and laughed at my slow understanding and clapped playfully, as if I was to be rewarded for finally paying attention.

I took a quick bow from my seat. "You have gluten-free bread!" It was hot from the oven. This was a first in Turkey. Gluten-free bread!

The waiter put a small dish of minced vegetable paste with olive oil on my table. "No gluten," he said, pointing to the dish.

Got it.

Bread. Hot bread. Hot gluten-free bread.

It had the best texture but tasted terrible. I didn't care. I slathered it with the vegetable paste and butter and ate every bite.

It was a perfect meal. I doubted that the sultans ate gluten-free bread, but that was a fair substitution.

I walked back to my hotel, slowly, my curfew is far earlier than Cinderella's: my goal is to be inside by dusk. I showered, hand-washed my dirty clothes in the sink and hung them to dry, then dressed for bed so I could write for a few hours from the comfort of my pajamas.

The electricity went out. Oh, no. Did we have an earthquake?

I stepped onto my balcony; the buildings around me had power. Okay, this happens regularly. A building will lose power for no apparent reason, then it pops back on in a half hour or so.

I sat on my bed and wrote for a few hours by the glow of my tablet. The electricity didn't come back on for most of the night, but that was okay, I didn't need it.

DAY 38: ISTANBUL: TRASH

"I s that her hair?" I asked the waiter as he came to my table to give me the check. I discreetly pointed to a table under the arch of the restaurant, indicating who I was talking about.

He looked quickly, then turned back to me. "Yes." He said it with a flat voice. He was younger than I was, maybe in his early forties.

"You think that's her real hair?" I asked.

He looked over at the Turkish woman with the gray hair sitting by herself. You know how some people have dreadlocks, where their hair is divided into portions, and each portion is wound around itself? This woman had something like that, only she had only one portion of hair, all nested into a giant web.

Dreadlock, singular?

It looked like a fat tube that extended from her head. She used both hands to reposition her nest, so it rested on her shoulder.

"Yes," the waiter said, flatly.

Okay. He thinks it's real hair. Was I fascinated or disgusted? I looked at the hair and worried I had reached the age where I lost my filter. Did traveling in Turkey age me? Was I staring at her the same way Turkish people stared at me?

I wanted to go up to her and ask, "Why?" Is this an exaggerated "bed head?" It looked heavy. Headache much? Did you plan this out, or just go with the natural flow of hair chaos? I wanted to take her photo but there was no way to do it covertly, so I just stared; I would regret this decision later.

Note to self: Next time take the photo.

I said to the waiter, "Please go over there and get a better look at her hair. I want to be sure it's real."

He stopped fiddling with the credit card machine. "You want me to go to her?"

"Yes. Please," I said. "I must understand."

He smirked, picked up a list of specials and walked over to the woman. He chatted with her for a moment, then handed her the menu.

I'd made a mistake coming to this restaurant, Hamdi. It was written up in Travel & Leisure magazine a few years ago as the best kebab restaurant in the city. Really, the best? The write-up made the food sound like a rare treat.

The spiced yogurt was amazing, the shish was regular. The price was more than double, $20 for lunch, which goes to show you the power of words.

I'd walked to this side of town to find the infamous Grand Bazaar, one of the oldest and largest marketplaces in the world, with over four thousand shops and more than sixty covered streets. I found my way there and entered "Gate Number 1" which felt like a win.

It was less of a bazaar and more like a mall, with marble floors and a roof overhead and occasional air conditioning. The vendors called to me as I passed by, as if they were a little angry that I wasn't buying. There weren't many people walking around.

I forced myself to take another loop so I might find something interesting in this old bazaar. But I gave up. Done. This wasn't my scene.

I left via a side door and was smack in the outer part of the bazaar. Partial tents shaded from the sun. Small shops spilled into the street. A steady parade of people walked by, all carrying bags from recent shopping. It was loud and dirty, and I was pleased to have stumbled onto it; these were my people.

I wondered if it was so filled with people because we are coming up on a holiday week in Turkey, or is it always this busy? I wandered the side streets for hours and bought some Turkish delight, rose flavor. My friend Kirsten was right, always go for the rose flavor.

After hours of getting happily lost in the maze of the outer bazaar, I'd found my way to the restaurant.

The waiter returned to my table and put my credit card into the machine.

He said, "It is real."

He didn't seem at all disgusted by it. "Do you like it?" I asked.

"No," he said, as if he had no opinion on anything to do with women.

"Have you ever seen this before?"

He thought for a moment. "No." He punched numbers into the machine and said, "Some people have their own style."

I nodded in agreement. "Would you let your wife wear her hair in a nest?"

"No," he said so fast that I laughed.

He smiled.

"Hmmm," I said. "Would you let your daughter wear her hair like that?"

He pulled off the first receipt and gave it to me with my card and shook his head, "No."

I watched as the woman readjusted her nest; it took both hands to find a position that wasn't pulling at the roots. "I'm afraid of her hair," I said.

"So am I," he said, quietly. He handed me the other receipt to sign.

I tucked my card and receipt into the pouch in my purse and signed his copy. "Thanks for your help."

He smiled, then turned and brought a menu to another table.

I had a list of things to do today, and the next thing on my list was to check out a neighborhood ten minutes away. It was a sunny day in Istanbul, and I was ready for a walk.

But, what's over there?

I followed the crowd. Sometimes I like to see where other people are going. The bridge! I'd found the bridge between the old part of Istanbul and the modern side of the city.

Now seemed like a good time to walk across. There were many other people walking across; I fell into a long line of bridge-crossers.

There were fishermen fishing off the bridge into the Golden Horn. They lined up, side by side, casting over the railing. I looked into one fisherman's tub of bait to see what he was using. Small dead fish. I couldn't tell if anyone had caught anything and lacked the language to ask. Nobody caught a fish while I walked past.

I followed the crowd, and entered a tunnel that led under the traffic and would set me where I could walk along the water.

There was a woman and a girl who might have been ten years old in the tunnel. They both had head scarves on, long sleeves and long pants. They were carrying a large plastic bag.

As I walked closer, I watched as the woman put the bag on the ground and ripped it open with a fast tear down the center. It was a bag of trash. Oh, they were sitting next to a dumpster. I wondered if they threw something away, accidently. The car keys. The TV remote. We've all had to dig through the garbage to find something we've lost.

The daughter sat on the ground and reached into the bag.

There were many of us walking past, a steady stream of people. I was the only foreigner.

The girl pulled out a piece of bread and put it into her mouth. She took enormous bites of it, quickly, as if someone might stop her from eating.

She was eating from the dumpster.

The steady stream of people slowed, watching. I wasn't the only one who was surprised by what I was seeing.

The mother reached into the dumpster for another bag while her daughter pulled out discarded pieces of flatbread from the open bag and piled them on her lap, a tower of partially eaten, dirty food.

This is not the first time I've been around people who were so hungry they would eat out of the trash; I've had hungry students over the years who would secretly pull other students' half-eaten food out of the garbage so they could eat it.

This was different. This was a child who was literally starving. It looked like they had a system in place, mom got the bags out and the girl collected the bread. They'd eaten trash before.

The bread was the big, round pieces of flatbread that come with fancy meals in restaurants. I looked around but didn't see a restaurant in my line of vision. Where did this trash come from?

The bread had bite marks along one side. The girl ate fast, not brushing the dirt off before she crammed more bread into her mouth and chewed as fast as she could.

She gorged on dirty bread and stockpiled more pieces. Did she have brothers and sisters she would share the newfound food with? A whole extended family?

As the crowd passed by, a number of people turned back to look. Yes. She was really eating garbage.

If I were going to eat garbage, I would hide behind the dumpster, but these two didn't care about being seen. Did they think they were invisible? Is that how we treat hunger in our societies, as if we can't see it?

I wanted to buy them food. I wanted to help. But they weren't asking for money and my attention might embarrass them, as they publicly stooped to a low point.

I walked away with the crowd but carried that image with me. That desperation. That hunger. How many children in our world are that hungry? How many children in my city are that hungry? How many children in the school where I teach are that hungry?

I vowed to find ways to add more snacks to my students' day. I would collect the untouched apples from the lunchroom for children to eat any time they were hungry. I would give more choices during snack time to be sure everyone had something to eat.

I recognized in myself how much easier it was to talk about the fashion faux pas of one than the hunger of another.

But I'm changing, slowly. I'm learning to witness all of it, no matter my own discomfort.

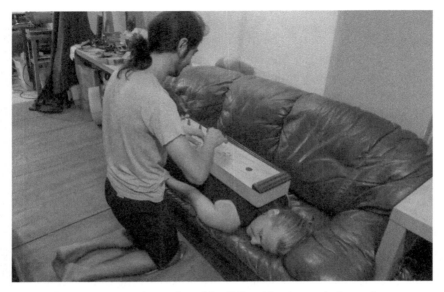

The instrument maker and musician Briken Aliu plays an instrument on the author's back as a form of healing.

Street musicians perform in Istanbul.

DAY 39: ISTANBUL: MUSIC

The instrument maker, Briken Aliu, said in halting English, "Please. Come. I want to try this you." He picked up the monochord instrument he had played for me in his workshop and walked into a different room.

I'd invented this instrument in my mind years ago when I was learning to play the guitar. Imagine an instrument where you could play any of the strings with no consideration of placement or tone, and it would sound good. I didn't know that an instrument like this existed.

It felt like someone took my idea of an invention, invented it and perfected it, and then on this day gave me a concert.

Imagined inventions do come true.

There were no finger positions to memorize. You could strum the strings in any order—it sounded good. If you wanted to go rogue and play every string together, it sounded good. If you played a few strings and plucked out a melody with the top strings—it sounded good.

Such a cool concept for a musical instrument. I wanted to learn more, but where were we going for this lesson?

"Please," the instrument maker said, kicking off his shoes in the living room and entering another room. "Come here."

I kicked off my shoes and followed behind him. He pointed to his queen-sized bed that had a beautiful quilt tucked under the sides. "Lay here."

Lie here? On his bed?

I met my music guide Riccardo Marenghi (https://www.facebook. com/riccardo.marenghi) He had over 190 five-star reviews for his music tour of Istanbul.

He is a working, well-respected jazz drummer who moved here from Italy and met the woman who would become his wife. They have one young daughter.

We sat and had a drink in a rooftop bar where he told me that his three-year-old daughter was starting in a Montessori school near their house.

He thought it was a great coincidence to find out I was a teacher in a Montessori school in New York. We talked about the philosophy of learning, and he showed me videos of his daughter's orientation in her new school where, during the drum circle, she got bored and went to work at a table.

We laughed at the video and he said, "She plays drums at home every day. This was not new for her."

The instrument maker was a good friend of my guide. We toured his workshop that was filled with guitars and harps and monotone instruments in various stages of assembly.

Being in the bedroom of the instrument maker seemed like an uncomfortable idea.

I lay on my stomach with my head on his pillow. He placed the instrument down the center of my back, crouched on the floor and began to play.

A man was playing a monotone instrument on my body in his bedroom.

At first the vibrations felt ticklish, and I giggled. I never heard of anyone having an instrument played on her back. If I'd heard of it before, I might think, "Oh, yes. This! I've read about this." It's difficult to catalogue something that's a true first.

I took a deep breath and tried to relax. It felt like the instrument was vibrating its sound deep into my body. I took a deeper breath and relaxed. It felt like I was in a deep meditation; the sound echoed through my body.

He strummed the instrument and as my brain tried to catch a tune with the strings, my body relaxed: it felt like I was sinking into the bed. My mind stopped. I was present, here, but it was as if I were in a dream state, while awake.

He stopped suddenly, lifted the instrument from me and turned to leave the room. "Get up slowly," he said.

We joined my guide in the living room.

I felt good. Why? How? I wanted to put words to this feeling. I said, "I feel like I've just finished a two-hour meditation."

The instrument maker smiled. He showed me examples of the instruments on the internet and asked if I went to a different "zone."

I didn't answer out loud; I was busy naming the experience in my head. "That was a different zone."

He explained that vibrations from an instrument can change your body's vibrations and help you heal or get to know yourself better.

We tried it again. I lay on the living room couch and my guide took a video. This time I didn't fight the experience and was pulled even deeper. He only played for one minute, but I felt like it had been far longer. I'd lost track of time.

My guide tried it too and when he got up, he had the same look on his face. Surprise. Relaxation. Peace.

He said, "I feel like I slept all night and now I am extra awake."

We thanked the instrument maker and continued our tour towards Taksim Square. It was eleven o'clock at night, and there were thousands of people outside. Friends. Families. People with heads covered. People showing a lot of skin. Children. Teens. Tourists. Locals.

"This is how Istanbul is," my guide said. "Everything is an opposite."

We got to the square where all of Turkey's major uprisings started. He pointed to where the million people who showed up for one demonstration had to stand, down the side streets, piled into the square, on top of buildings lining the square. Imagine a million people demonstrating.

You can't visit a place of violence without feeling the weight of it. What if?

What if someone started an uprising right now at this very minute, and I just happened to be a tourist walking through the square at the moment of uprising. Then what?

That kind of civil unrest hasn't been a part of my life in the States. Sure, I've heard about Turkey's problems over the years, but sitting in my pajamas at night and eating dinner while hearing about the unrest of another country on the news is different than standing in the spot where everything started.

People died here while defending their country or wanting change.

I looked over my shoulder to be sure a revolt wasn't starting behind me.

Nope. No revolts.

My guide explained, "Gas canisters are the size of a can of Coca-Cola."

I didn't know that.

He said the government used so much tear gas that the canisters were shin-high throughout the square. He told a story of how one night he was walking home, and something happened, he couldn't breathe.

He called his Turkish wife, who said matter-of-factly, "Someone must have used gas in the area. Keep walking. You'll be fine in twenty minutes."

My guide turned to me. "She wasn't at all alarmed that I had walked into a dangerous area and couldn't breathe. She just said to keep walking."

We walked back along the main walking street, Istiklal Caddesi. There were so many people that you couldn't see the road.

"A carpet of people," my guide said.

We stopped and listened to live music, some on the street, some in bars. We listened to a New Orleans-style jazz band in a bar called Bova that was so good, I think a hotel in NOLA might want to hire them full time. The musicians greeted my guide by name, and after visiting for a while, we went back outside.

There were even more people walking along Istiklal Avenue, or Independence Avenue.

"I'm going to show you something now," he said and turned off to a side street.

It was a quiet street. I was glad I wore my sneakers for the tour, it's challenging to walk on cobblestones in sandals.

At the end of the block, two women leaned out of a window and called to the men on the street. Several men stopped to talk to them. We rounded the corner and there were several more windows with women leaning out, calling to men.

After we passed, I asked the guide how old he thought the women were. All red-light districts I've seen before had young women. These women looked older.

He laughed and looked at me. "They were men."

I said slowly, "They were men."

"Yes."

"They didn't look like men," I said.

He said, "They work all day to look like women. They are very good at it."

I've seen transvestites before, even went to a transvestite brunch show with friends a few months ago, but those men at the brunch looked like men who looked like women.

The people leaning out of those windows looked like women.

I said, "Who are their customers? Men or women?"

He shrugged. "I don't know. Whoever pays."

I walked on quietly. "How much does it cost?"

"I don't know."

"Do they get a lot of customers?"

"I don't know."

"Do you know anyone who ever went...upstairs?"

"No."

I was beginning to understand that Istanbul really was a city of opposites. There are women who must remain covered up and there are men who dress like women who aren't covered up.

My view of Turkey as a conventional country was eroding. The people who make up Turkey are as varied as any other place.

My guide offered to walk me back to my hotel at the end of the night, so I didn't have to walk alone along the dark streets, but it was already 1:00 AM and I didn't mind taking a taxi.

"Are you sure?" he said. "I can go with you in the taxi and go home from there."

He lived in the other direction with his wife and daughter; I could take a taxi.

He talked to the driver and told him in Turkish where to take me.

I looked up the cost of a taxi earlier in the day because I'd thought about getting a ride to this side of town for my tour: the cost was 23 to 30 lira. I didn't take a taxi earlier but was glad to know the price now.

We chose a taxi stand that was closer to my hotel than where we first met, and since the roads were empty at this time of night, I figured it would cost less than 20 lira.

The stores were just closing. Imagine being open till 1:00 AM every night. How many shifts of workers do they need every day? One. Probably only one very long shift with no days off during the week. I've heard about the long hours from various workers.

We got to my neighborhood, but the driver couldn't find my hotel, so I asked him to stop so I could walk the rest of the way.

The meter on his car was strange. I couldn't understand the numbers. They started at 1.2 and only went up to 1.3. Was I being charged in dollars or euros?

"How much?" I asked.

He picked up a calculator and punched in the number "60."

Sixty lira?

We tourists are warned about this scam. Taxi drivers take advantage of foreigners who don't understand the currency and charge them inflated prices.

I started yelling in English, "No." I pointed to the meter. "Show me on the meter."

He shrugged his shoulders and smiled, indicating he forgot to start the meter.

I knew he couldn't understand my words, but my tone was crystal clear. "How dare you. I'm not giving you sixty lira. You're getting twenty lira, which is more than the cost of the ride."

I opened the taxi and stepped out. I reached inside and handed him the 20 lira bill.

"No," he said, upset. "Need..." He pointed to the calculator.

I didn't know how to call the police on my phone, or I would have. I raised my voice. "Call the police," I said. "Now. Call the police."

He said in a high-pitched squeal, "More money. I need more."

"Not from me," I said. I slammed the door and walked away. I might have looked more like a badass if I knew where my hotel was, but I had to hit a link on Google maps and spin around a few times to figure out which direction to walk.

The taxi driver circled around and stopped next to me. "Lady. More money. I need more money."

I didn't like that he was following me. Luckily, I had an audience; the man from the fish shop sat outside hoping for customers. At 1:00 AM he's hoping for customers?

I yelled at the driver, "Call the police," and walked away. "Call the police now," I shouted back to him.

The taxi driver sat in the cab a half a block away, watching me. I found the hotel and used my key to get inside, making sure to lock the door behind me.

I climbed up the three floors to my room and locked myself inside. I texted my guide about the injustice.

"Yes," he texted back. "That happens."

A tasty find: gluten-free baklava.

A young worker stands embarrassed as a woman shops for underwear at an outdoor market.

DAY 40: ISTANBUL: IMPOSSIBLE

"He said to turn right, right?" I asked myself.

I answered myself, "I think so."

I turned right and walked along the sidewalk next to the sea. Seagulls flew over the waves, surfers of the wind. Waves hit the rocks in a polite game of tag, tag—you're it, tag—you're it, again. Couples walked hand in hand, slowly, as if they had all the time in the world, while teen boys walked side by side at a fast pace and called out to the teen girls who hung together on boulders next to the water, waiting to be noticed.

There was a circle of people surrounding a music player of some kind. They appeared to be strangers, but all danced together. A line dance in a circle and everyone knew the steps. I watched as people ran to join the group; either they loved this song, or they loved this dance, or they wanted to be a part of something on a random sidewalk on the Asian side of Istanbul.

Istanbul is a city with a split personality. It is so big that a 20-minute ferry across the Bosporus Strait connects you to a different continent in the same city: from Europe to Asia. On paper about 15 million people live in Istanbul, but locals insist that there are at least

16 million people living within the city limits: that's twice the size of New York City as a comparison.

I was afraid to come to Istanbul, fearing it was too large to conquer. How would I find my way? What part of the city should I stay in? I didn't research this big city before I started my trip, what would I do there?

But when I visited the sisters in Atabey, they thought I should give it a try. Maybe just a few days? The librarian's eyes lit up when she talked about Istanbul, and I thought that if I could figure out where to stay, a safe place with many things to do around it, then I would go.

That's always the first step to any place I visit. Where can a solo woman traveler stay and feel safe? It takes hours of research to find the right area, then a hotel or guest house that's within a half a mile from the good area. I don't mind walking if the area is considered safe and interesting.

I met two women from Turkey on the ferry ride back from Greece a few weeks ago. They also insisted that I go to Istanbul.

"But where should I stay?" I asked.

They spoke in rapid Turkish to each other. Then one said, "Stay as close to the Blue Mosque as you can. That way if you are lost, you can ask anyone in the city, and they will be able to direct you."

That was a really good idea. I followed their advice and got a room near the Blue Mosque.

I talked to the owner of the guest house where I was staying. I told him about my taxi ride the night before and how the taxi driver inflated the price of the ride by 300 percent. He listened to my story and said I did the right thing, knowing the fare and paying him the 20 lira.

He had this advice for future taxi rides:

"The next time, before you get into a taxi, you must read the driver's face. If he does not have a good face, do not get in his taxi. I have seen a lot of bad faces on taxi drivers. Don't get in the wrong car."

Back home when there is a row of taxis, a customer is expected to hire the first taxi in the line. Not so here: the customer can choose any taxi for any reason.

This helped me understand when I was on my way to Cappadocia, and those two taxi drivers stood in the rain as they extolled their virtues so I would choose one of them for a ride. In Turkey, choosing a taxi is a matter of choice and a compliment.

I told the owner of my hotel that I was a little worried that that driver would come back here, looking for me.

The owner said, "If you see that taxi driver again, I want to talk to him. I have some questions for him."

I smiled both inside and outside. Many of the Turkish men I meet are willing to take on the role of "helpful big brother," and the help is always welcome.

He gave me another tip: the best ice cream in the city was on the Asian side of Istanbul.

Take a ferry. Turn right. Walk fifteen minutes on the sidewalk. When you come to a place where there is a coffee shop on a high hill, climb the hill and ask them where the Moda ice cream shop is. They will direct you.

Though his directions weren't as precise as a map program on the internet, they worked. I bought two scoops of pistachio ice cream and found a table with a view of the sea, in the shade where I could enjoy my dessert. Smooth. Sweet. Pistachio. Cold.

I only had a few days left until I returned home. No. Don't think about that now. Stay present. Pay attention. Taste that pistachio. Hear the birds? See the sunlight hitting the water. Feel the chill of the ice cream on a hot day.

This treat was worth the continental hop.

Before I left New York, I thought the one crown jewel of the trip would be if I could find gluten-free baklava; I knew there wasn't a chance.

Gluten-free dough is a challenge to make; alternative flours make a dry dough. I attended baking classes from a woman in Denver years ago who would make gluten-free cookie dough, then refrigerate it overnight. The next day she'd bring the dough to room temperature and add more liquid and repeat the process until the dough reached the right consistency.

Rather than learn this wise method, I stopped making cookies when I was diagnosed with celiac disease.

To make baklava, you have to roll each individual sheet of dough as thin as possible, then smear it with a honey mixture, and then roll out another sheet of dough until it is uber-thin, and put it on top of the first, until layer after layer makes a stack.

A food guide I booked a tour with sent me a message on WhatsApp asking if he could help me in any way before our tour. Was there something I was wanting? Something special?

I messaged him back that he would earn a "Gold Star" if he could find me gluten-free baklava.

He sent me a link to a place across the Golden Horn. He told me to ask for the gluten-free version: glutensiz.

Wait. Really? Someone makes gluten-free baklava?

From the bridge it's about a ten-minute walk to the shop in the trendy Karaköy neighborhood. I found the place, easily, and paid for my dessert first, as the website mentioned.

Karaköy Güllüoğlu is a large pastry shop where giant displays of baklava sit behind glass like precious jewels. Some flavors are cut into small rectangles, others are cut into giant triangle wedges. I couldn't read the flavors or combinations, but they seemed to be more organic, meaning there wasn't a bright red-dyed selection called, "Cherry Berry."

I got someone's attention and said, "Glutensiz?" and was pointed in the right direction. Which kind did I want, pistachio or walnut?

There are gluten-free choices. Really?

A worker packed two squares of each into a little box and I sat on their patio and opened the box slowly and took a bite. Sweet. Flaky. Nutty. I took another bite to be sure. Yes. This. A perfect creation in the world of gluten-free baking.

And so I added another entry to my list of impossible things realized: gluten-free baklava.

Thanks, Turkey.

DAY 40: COUNTDOWN TO GOING HOME

After graduating with my associate's degree in 1985, I lived in Europe for several years, first in London and then in Amsterdam. When it was time to return to the United States and my childhood home, I threw away all of my tattered clothes and filled my backpack with enormous bars of Dutch chocolate and one-foot balls of artisan cheeses; my priorities had changed.

On the airplane I had to fill out customs forms that made me promise that I had no food in my luggage. If I had known earlier that it was a problem to bring food home, I wouldn't have tried.

Too late. I checked every box: no food.

My plan, if they found the cheese and chocolate, was to blame my friends Susan and her children, whom I'd been staying with, and claim that she must have secretly stuffed my backpack with Dutch delicacies.

In the end I wasn't stopped in customs, so I didn't need to tell a tall tale.

European treats weren't available on store shelves in those days, so the gifts were well received.

Chocolate for you.

Cheese for you.

Chocolate for you.

Cheese for you.

Many things are different in 2019; I had little reason to lug gifts home from Turkey, other than a few evil-eye amulets and handwoven towels. After a basic internet search, I could buy Turkish trays, small glass teacups and even my favorite white cheese with a click of a button. A large block of sheep's cheese would arrive at my door the day after I got home, with free shipping.

On this trip, I wouldn't carry anything forbidden in my suitcase, like spices or open containers of food, because when flying out of Turkey—they hand-check every bag.

I started organizing my belongings for the trip home.

Home? I dreaded going home.

Something happened to me on this trip; I lost sight of home. It was as if I were Hansel and Gretel and refused to follow the breadcrumbs back to my house, wanting instead to check out a new path, knowing home was there if I wanted it. Sure, my life was waiting for me to return, laden with stories and new recipes, but something bubbled up inside of me. I was a stranger to myself; I wasn't ready to go home, and I couldn't articulate why. It was as if my priorities had changed again, only this time it wasn't about swapping my clothing for food. My new priorities chose traveling over home.

That was a big leap.

Normally I'm ready to go home at the end of a trip, and tired and maybe even a little bored from the discomforts of the road.

Not this time.

What if my life were a locked cage?

Normally when I return from a trip, I look forward to sitting in my car and having the radio buttons set to my favorite stations, and showering in my bathroom and wearing clothes that hadn't fit into my suitcase, and reconnecting with my people and sleeping in my bed.

Not this time.

Oh, I know, we all sadden when the vacation is over, but something deep inside of me wanted to keep on going. Keep traveling. Keep learning. Keep meeting new people. My home was no longer the house on the creek—my home had become adventure itself. I mourned the moment my travels finished.

It scared me, this lack of homesickness.

I imagined cutting the string to my life and saying, "I used to have a big house on a creek." The past tense fit comfortably into my present life.

Why?

I tried to think positively about returning home. I would find weekend getaways to feed my need of adventure. I vowed to meet new people from different cultures from the comfort of my own town, it would be my new definition of armchair travel: I would get to know the people around me.

My friends planned a big party for me a few days after I returned to help with my "reentry," or the returning home after the fun of traveling.

And there was a man. We'd met on the internet before I left for Turkey. He was an artist and lived about twenty minutes away. We didn't have enough time to figure out if we would be a good couple, but we had four dates and found that our time together was easy. He had a history of interesting travel, which was a plus: he understood my desire to immerse myself in a different culture.

But after a few weeks of hanging out, he was torn: half of him wanted an invitation to join me and the other half wanted to forbid me from going.

Neither option worked for me, which was why I didn't let our time get serious. I didn't want to have to check in with him or worry about him worrying about me while I was on the road.

So we parted without promises. He would keep dating; I would travel.

He read my writings that I posted for friends and family and emailed me from time to time, reminding me to live fully in the moment and enjoy it all.

A few days before my flight home, he emailed and asked if we could get together when I got back. He said I should take as much time as I needed, but that he would love to see me.

Time with him was just the distraction I needed. Mind you, I did like him. He was cute and smart and funny, an awe-inspiring artist.

I would get home at 2:00 AM after twenty-four hours of travel. I invited him to meet me that same day in the late afternoon, warning that I had no food in the house, but that he could come and hang out.

He stayed three days, and then I stayed at his house on and off for the next few weeks. He gave me painting lessons, the kind where I put a blob of orange paint on a board and said, "Honey, could you make this look better?" and he'd kiss me and with a few dabs of paint, make the piece of fruit I was trying to paint look edible.

With him at my side I could paint!

My friend Sonia visited from far away. She glowered at me after dinner when he went to the bathroom: "What are you thinking?"

I was having fun.

My sister Heather met him and thought he was different from the men I normally spend time with.

Was that a good thing?

My friend Lynda found him to be completely charming. She bought one of his paintings; it hangs in her living room, a gem on her wall.

The artist and I traveled to New York City a few weeks after my return, and on the first day he introduced me to his people as "The Best Girlfriend in the World." The very next day something in him changed. He criticized me constantly and disagreed with everything I said.

I wasn't sure if he was tired, or tired of me. I asked, but in the asking he got angry and that led to a night of him yelling for being questioned while he was tired. I watched him as if from far away, sad to see this side of him and thinking that Sonia was right, which was almost as alarming.

So we ended there, my bridge between adventure and home crumbled.

The questions I was asking myself as I packed to fly home from Istanbul floated in front of me again. Where is home? What matters most? When do I feel most alive?

I was willing to ask the questions but didn't know how to formulate the answers.

Not yet.

Logs of Turkish delight in a shop window.

A worker carries a tray to deliver tea to workers in the market.

DAY 41: ISTANBUL: WALK

"No," the guard yelled at me. He held his arm in front of me so I couldn't enter the "fast track" at the Basilica Cistern. "No," he yelled again just to be sure the shock value of hearing his loud voice next to my face got the full effect.

Man, why is it that I always find the angry guards?

I showed him my swanky 15-day Museum Pass (I bought it for a near fortune), which boasts a fast entrance to many museums in Turkey.

The guard did not appreciate me showing him my 15-day Museum Pass.

He yelled louder. I backed away, then saw a sign in English that said this site was excluded from the Museum Pass.

Good to know.

A Turkish man approached me. "Don't leave, don't you want to go inside?"

I shrugged; did he see how that guard yelled at me? I really hate to be yelled at. I said, "I can't use my museum pass here."

"I work here," he said, lowering his voice. "I can get you in."

I hesitated. Maybe I could enter through the staff entrance. That would be so cool!

"Yeah?" I said. "What would it cost?"

"Nothing," he said. "No charge."

That's my favorite price.

He said, "I'm working, so I can't get you in right now. But I know a guy and he can get you in for free." He started looking around for his friend.

Really?

My friend Linda had sent me a message, asking me to please stay safe, and here I was, conspiring to breaking and entering to get past the four hundred people standing in line. (No exaggeration.) (Okay. A little exaggeration.)

I have a strong adversity to illegal entering. I backpedaled and left my scam artist. He couldn't believe I was walking away from a sure thing.

I said, "No, thanks. Not interested. I'm going now. Goodbye. No thanks. No thanks. No. No. No. Goodbye."

I can walk fast when I'm escaping drama; he finally turned back.

It's always interesting to see what gimmick will get my attention: empathy for not getting into the museum worked. I'm so easy.

Earlier I was wandering around an old bazaar where Bill Clinton shopped when he came to town. I wouldn't have known that Bill shopped there, but I was buying a small necklace from a small shop and the owner bragged about Bill shopping there on three different occasions.

I told the owner, "Bill's a good guy."

I thought it was a creative way to let the owner know that I was American and knew my former presidents, but instead the owner shook my hand and said he was glad to meet a friend of Bill's.

He insisted I drink a cup of tea with him, and there's this strange cultural norm in Turkey that if you refuse a cup of tea while shopping, you're a cad.

I'm not Bill Clinton's friend and I don't like tea.

Yeah, whatever. I drank the damn tea and heard about how Bill was such a nice guy.

I tried to fix my creative mistake by telling the shop owner that I was a kindergarten teacher, but it was too late. Any friend of Bill's was excluded from bargaining rights: I paid full price for the necklace. But don't worry, the next time I see Bill, I'm going to make him pay me the difference.

So after that purchase I was walking up a very long staircase outside the shop, and a man walked next to me. He said, "Where are you from?"

There are scam artists who work the square who ask that question all day long. I said, "Everywhere."

He laughed.

Usually the scammers didn't laugh.

I said, "Where are you from?"

He said, "Everywhere."

I laughed and said, "We're neighbors!"

He laughed and said, "I'm not one of those guys who works the square. Do you need help finding anything?"

I knew where I was going so declined his help. A few minutes later I wished I had asked him about the guys who work the square. What exactly was their job description?

I wandered down to the Galata Bridge and people-watched for a while, then got an idea. I pulled up a list of museums on my phone that are part of the Museum Pass program. The Mosaic Museum was on the list.

I love mosaics.

I had to walk all the way back to the area around my hotel, but that's okay, I like to walk.

There was nobody in line at the Mosaic Museum. I flashed my Museum Pass and was waved in, VIP style, although the glory was muted without a line of people to cut in front of. There were only five other people in the whole entire microscopic museum. I congratulated myself on finding a better place to walk around.

After I got my fill of the history of mosaics: discovering them, relocating them and cleaning them with a mixture of hot air (really) and the occasional chemicals, I got this idea that I ought to go to the Spice Market. How could I miss seeing the spice market, again?

It was on the other side of town, where I was earlier. That's okay, I like to walk.

The Spice Market was closed as some people are still on holiday. They're probably at home, making delicious spicy dishes and relishing the fact that the rest of us can't spice our food because they're closed.

Several streets around the Spice Market were open and selling goods. Since my days in Istanbul were numbered with only two more full days after today, I felt braver and took some photos of the people and the places around town.

And then when I was done with that, I found my way back to my side of town.

It's okay, I like to walk.

~

Photo next page: Istiklal Avenue, or Independence Avenue, Istanbul.

190-year-old brass containers of homemade jam. You bring your own container and scoop out as much as you want.

Cheeses numbered clockwise from the top: #1: Izmir Tulum Cheese #2: Isli Cerkez, smoked cheese—would eat this one again. #3: Corek Otu-- cheese with black seeds. Not bad. #4: A very favorite cheese, Beyaz from cow or sheep. There are many different varieties. #5: Tulum cheese with chestnuts. Fermented in goat skin sack and placed in a cave. Luxury cheese. (Not a favorite.) #6: Kasar cheese. Like parmesan.

DAY 42: ISTANBUL: FOOD

"Here are three kinds of *lokum* (which means morsel), or Turkish delight for you to taste," my food guide Emre öğüdücü (Instagram @foodtour_istanbul_emre) said, setting a sample plate on our table. "Try this one first. It's a plain one."

He lifted a finger, as if he were going to suggest something else, but it was too late. I popped the whole piece of candy into my mouth. Oh, this was good. Wow.

Wait, is this what Turkish delight is supposed to taste like?

We were in the candy store, Haci Bekir, which was started by a man named Ali Muhiddin in the late 1700s when the sultan demanded a new kind of candy. It's one of those defining moments when the sultan voices his displeasure and you must improvise, quickly.

Ali came up with a mixture of gelatin and sugar and water that would stay fresh tasting for a long time and had just a hint of sweetness. The sultan loved it. At first it was candy fit only for a sultan, but over time other bakers came up with their own recipes fit for the rest of us.

Chefs and bakers have been copying those improvised recipes for years. According to my guide, there are over seven thousand bakeries in Istanbul, but not all of them make lokum.

The copycat candies other bakers invented come out too hard or too sweet and stick to your teeth. I'd tried many of the different candies at different shops searching for one I liked. I was told that this was an acquired taste, so I kept sampling.

We were sitting in the original bakeshop where Ali first came up with the concept, which explains why these candies were superior.

The taste of the first sample was subtle, the texture soft and chewy. This piece had a hint of pistachio flavoring. It wasn't sticky or hard. This was different.

"This is amazing," I said, picking up the next piece.

Before my food guide could say anything, I had the whole piece of rose lokum in my mouth.

This was so different from the other rose-flavored treats I'd tried. This one had just a hint of rose, and the texture was a little chewy, but nothing stuck to my teeth. Though I was far from an expert, this piece of rose lokum might be the best thing in candy.

"This might be the best thing in candy," I said as I reached for the next piece.

Food Guide put his hand over the last piece before I could gobble it. "Wait. Clear your palate. Drink this first."

It was a dark drink. Juice? I could taste apricot, but he said it wasn't juice.

He explained that long ago people used to dry fruits like apricots, plums and tamarind. Over the winter when fruit was tough to come by, they would add water and sugar to the dried fruits and let it steep until the water was an infusion that was thicker than juice.

This was a sample of *serbet*, a drink from dried sweet fruits. Thick. Sweet. Apricot.

I was instructed to take a small bite of the last candy. I ate a small piece then immediately went for another small piece.

"Oh, good." My guide smiled. "You like this one!"

We had started the tour at a cheese shop. There were six samples, including my favorite white sheep's cheese, *beyaz*, and I sampled them all. I liked the smoked cheese but could do without the *tulum* cheese that was cured in a goatskin, deep in a cave where the enzymes from the skin help to ferment the cheese. Beyaz cheese was still my favorite; I left the other samples on the plate.

He asked me repeatedly if I would eat all of the cheeses.

I invited him to join me. I'd eaten cheese every single day for six weeks and didn't feel like eating cheese that I didn't like. I'd become a cheese snob.

It was easy for me to leave cheese on the plate, but this candy—here was something I'd eat all day. At home I ate very little sugar; while traveling I ate as much sugar as I wanted. That was my balanced approached to health.

This last sample was made with carrot paste, which might classify as a vegetable on a sliding scale of nutrition. Chewy. Sweet. Craveable.

I bought small sample boxes of each to take home.

When the tour was over, we continued walking around because my food guide's next tour wasn't for a few hours. He showed me old churches, a theater where Louis Armstrong performed, and walked me through restaurants and coffee shops that were built in the alleyways between buildings.

No wasted space, kind of like my time in Turkey: no wasted space.

After we parted, I found another Rumi museum that accepted my Museum Pass. Their collection was sparse, and I felt none of the connection I felt at the museum in Konya. Another reminder to myself that my trip to see the real thing was time well spent.

I walked around in a state of melancholy. I was in Istanbul, my new favorite city in the world. I knew my way around a few basic areas. I could find my favorite foods and greet sites by name. I'd learned how to walk along the tram tracks to get by a crowd until you hear that horn and then return to the busy sidewalk. I had favorite restaurants, favorite fruit stands, favorite cheeses and now, favorite candies.

There was a little café on my walk home with an open seat. I ordered a bottle of water and watched people walk by. The colors of clothing. The styles. The tones of voices. Carrying bags? Hurried or relaxed? Do the children look happy?

Yes. They do.

I had two nights left in this city. What did I want to do tonight?

My first choice was to sit on my balcony and watch the moon come up over the Golden Horn.

So I did.

DAY 43: ISTANBUL: SELF-CARE

An attendant unwrapped my towel from around my body and stretched it out on the heated marble.

She said, "You lay. Five."

I wasn't naked, I was wearing a pair of black underwear that the hamam provided. There were other women in the sauna-like treatment room, all of us wore matching undies. I went to lie on my back, the attendant patted her stomach. I turned onto my stomach.

For my last full day in Istanbul, I treated myself to a hamam near my hotel. A little self-care seemed like the perfect way to spend a few hours. Since I went to my first hamam a few weeks ago, I figured I knew what to expect.

Not at all.

This one had a giant octagon-shaped marble slab that was big enough to have eight women worked on at different areas. There were four other women in the room with me, all in various stages of treatment.

This was the women's area and all of the attendants were women.

We were each given a space near the edge of the marble slab. An attendant wearing fancier black underwear and a black bra worked on a woman lying in the area next to mine. They chatted in Turkish while the attendant scrubbed her down with a coarse mitt.

Other women were resting after a treatment or covered in a mountain of soap bubbles as they got their soapy massage. It was sort of like "Girls' Night" except we didn't know each other, and we didn't talk to each other, but there was something about having other women around me that made the experience feel festive, like a self-care party.

A woman came into the room with the number 40 dangling from her bra. She introduced herself and after speaking for a while, she decided that I was deaf and started pantomiming. This made it so much easier to understand her. Why hadn't I thought of this before?

I let her know that I spoke English.

She spoke to me in rapid Turkish that ended with her voice going up. Oh, she was asking me a question.

"No Turkish," I said.

Her mouth opened in surprise.

"No Turkish?" she said.

"No Turkish."

There was a much fancier hamam on the square near the Blue Mosque, maybe that's where most of the English-speakers go.

She exfoliated me quickly, as if it were a race and she was bound to win. I wondered if she felt accomplished that only half of my body was rubbed clean? As she started the soap massage, she sang to me, quietly, as if the two were related: soap, sing. Soap, sing. I don't know if the song was related to massage or if she was singing the recipe for making bread, but it sounded like a lullaby and I accepted it as such.

It was lovely, lying on the heated marble slab while getting massaged and sung to. I wondered if she would have sung to me if she thought I could understand her words?

Maybe there is no bad hamam experience.

Feeling rejuvenated, I made my way back to the Spice Market to see if it was open. The crowds were thick. Why were there so many people walking around? I walked down the hill, looking for the spice stalls. There were even more people. Today is the last day of the big holiday; are these typical crowds or holiday crowds?

People behind me pressed forward as we shuffled towards the Spice

Market. Then the crowd in front of me stopped. If the people behind you are moving forward and the people in front of you have stopped, you are caught in the middle.

Too tight. We were all being squeezed into juice. There were strangers pressing me from all four sides. We stood still, squished into one giant, sweaty pod. I wasn't afraid of getting robbed or annoyed by the pressing of bodies around me, but for the first time in my life I wondered if I was claustrophobic. I wanted to scratch and claw my way out of what felt like confinement.

There was no easy way out of the dense crowd.

I concentrated on keeping my breathing calm and steady, and moved my attention to observing the people around me. Nobody else seemed uncomfortable with the close proximity. I tried to pretend it was like a group hug, but that didn't work. This was more like a vice grip, and I wanted out. Now.

I wanted out now.

Six young men linked up, each put his hands on the shoulders of the man in front of him and the leader gently pushing his way forward, towards a side street. It was working; slowly the crowd made way for them.

I didn't link up with the shoulders of the man in front of me, but I stood so close to him we were practically wearing the same shirt. I tailed them and managed to wiggle through to a side street where there were still too many people, but at least the crowd was moving.

Okay. That was a little better. I could breathe again.

I didn't know if the lack of space was more intolerable because I'd just finished my relaxing hamam experience, but I had a sudden need for space. Space around me. More space.

And so I walked slowly, from street to street, always choosing the way with the least number of people. I continued moving away from my hotel in a direction I hadn't walked before.

That's what I like about travel, I can forge my own path depending on my mood. If I choose to be around more people, I can write that into my travel-script. If I prefer to be around fewer people, I can turn up a street where the shops are closed.

After hours and hours of discovering a new city, I can head back for a nap or continue exploring. Every decision I make while on the road suits what I want to do. After a school year teaching from a small classroom where my students' needs go before my needs, following my whims is the ultimate freedom.

For the rest of my teaching career I could choose to live a summer of adventure. I held on to that promise—I can travel every summer.

And so the plan for next summer was set: I would travel. Making this promise to myself made this ending easier to bear.

I came upon a restaurant that had a menu posted. Hey, wait, these are the best prices I've seen in the whole country. I found a table and looked out at the traffic. Is it busier today because the holiday is over?

The restaurant was next to a 4-lane road with busy traffic. I didn't mind cars; I didn't want to be around people.

The waiter approached my table and said, "Yes, Mom. What like you?"

Calling me Mom was a sign of respect; how many years before the young will change the greeting to, "Yes, Grandma. What like you?"

I smiled into his kindness and ordered. A large plate of meze—carrot salad, roasted eggplant, hummus, seaweed, pickled veggies, broccoli, double the yogurt, extra cucumber slices, hold the *muhammara*, no bread. And then lamb shish and spiced yogurt. For dessert, rice pudding with mango and a cup of tea.

This was my last supper. It was too much food for one meal, but since I'd be leaving first thing in the morning and then traveling for over twenty-four hours to get home to New York, I ordered every one of my favorite foods.

The meze was fresh. The shish was hot. The rice pudding was the creamiest I'd had yet. It was the best restaurant meal of the entire trip.

The waiter brought the bill. "You understand Turkey food, yes, Mom?"

When I left, I tipped him as if he were my son.

DAY 44: ISTANBUL TO NY: END

"I thought I was stronger than you are," the owner of the guest house said as he took my suitcase from me at the bottom of three flights of narrow stairs.

He propped my suitcase next to the front window.

We sat for a few minutes and talked about the first rain I'd seen in six weeks.

"You're lucky," he said.

I smiled, thinking about the many parts of my six weeks in Turkey that went better than planned and made me feel lucky. "Yes. I am."

He told me about the guests who would arrive in the next few days. A woman from Sweden, a couple from Russia and some friends from Spain.

"So I got injured last night," I said. I was the only one staying in the guest house last night. I had the phone numbers of the owner and his nephew in case I needed anything.

He raised his eyebrows. "You got hurt?"

"I hit my ankle on the bathroom door. There was a lot of blood. I almost called you to take me to the hospital."

"I'm so sorry," he said, exhaling slowly. "Those things can happen."

"Nothing to worry about," I said. "I cleaned it up as well as I could."

He nodded slowly. Turkish men are good at not showing surprise.

I didn't know I was bleeding for almost ten minutes. Only noticed it when there were ants all over the room.

What? Why? More ants, again?

Why were the ants back?

The first time the ants took over my room, they were drawn in by my small bag of almonds. The cleaning lady, Nellie, told me through the translation program that ants liked almonds.

Okay. No more almonds in my room.

The second time the ants came to visit, they were summoned by a small bread board that I bought during my food tour. The board was covered in a natural oil; the ants loved that. Nellie scrubbed the board with hand soap from my bathroom and then cleaned my room from top to bottom, again.

Now the ants had returned. Why? Why were they here? I was leaving in the morning and didn't want to take ants home with me.

I thought the red stuff all over the floor was cherry syrup and I stood there wondering where the syrup came from. I didn't buy anything red, did I?

It was only during the investigation of how much syrup was on the floor that I figured it out: the red was coming from my ankle. I had caught it in the bathroom door earlier but didn't know that blood was a part of the injury.

Oh, right. Blood. My last lesson in Turkey came with the realization that ants love blood.

My blood.

The ants must have been close by. As soon as they smelled the first drop, they sounded the alarm, "American blood!"

It was a quandary, kill the ants first or clean up the blood first?

I stuck my foot into a plastic bag and used a hairband to keep it in place to contain the blood.

I had nothing to wipe up the mess but toilet paper, which left white wisps and looked even messier. I cleaned and killed ants, and, in the end, the room looked like I'd invited over twenty friends with very dirty feet.

I cleaned some more. And some more, until it looked almost presentable. The wound kept opening so I slept with my foot wrapped in toilet paper with a clean plastic bag held on by that hair tie.

You don't realize how noisy a plastic bag is until you try to sleep with one on your foot. Crinkle. Crinkle.

In the morning, the toilet paper washed off the wound in the shower.

Rather than explain this to Nellie, I told the owner, who speaks excellent English.

"I will let her know."

On the way to the airport I fell asleep and was transported in my dreams to my house. So when I woke up and I was at the Istanbul airport, I was excited to still be in the arms of travel.

To enter the airport, I had to go through an x-ray security checkpoint. Okay, no problem. Then to enter the line at the check-in counter for Turkish Airways, you must answer the famed questions that countries in the Middle East ask.

"Who packed your bags? Where did you leave them after you packed them? Could anyone have put anything into the bags? Did you offer to carry anything for someone else?"

After I passed this level of security, I waited on a long, snaking line so I could check in. I gave the agent at the ticket counter my passport and she studied it carefully: "What is your name? What city are you from? What is your birthdate? When did you arrive in Turkey? How many days were you here?" and then she checked me in for the flight and took my suitcase.

The duty-free shops at this new Istanbul airport are, in their own right, as big as an airport. I took a stroll through the perfume area, but my favorite scent is clean, and I don't need perfume to manage that one.

A medium bag of M&Ms cost $15. When did duty-free shops become more expensive than shopping at home?

I made my way towards my gate; every passenger on my flight had to go through these next steps:

I had to put my carry-on bag through another x-ray machine to enter the gate area. Then there was another passport security screening so I could answer questions about who I am and where I am from, again. I wondered if they were comparing my answers. Were they searching for people traveling with stolen passports?

Then a few steps away, there was another passport screening interview. I resisted the urge to act surprised that they cared so much about my passport; this wasn't a game.

A man in uniform sharpened his look as he flipped through my passport.

"What day did you enter the country?" he asked.

"July 3rd," I said.

"What city did you enter from?"

"Istanbul."

"No," he said. "Wrong answers."

I stood looking at him. That was all I had. "Izmir. July 3rd."

He stared back. His face hardened and he shook his head back and forth.

I'd passed this test at the other stops in the airport, how could this answer suddenly be so...wrong?

"I came here on July 3rd and I've been here the whole time," I said, racking my brain for something I might have forgotten.

"Wrong." He announced it as if I were at a spelling bee and was now disqualified.

Was this what my friend's husband had warned me about? They said that women were detained at the airport and then jailed at the end of their trip. I'd forgotten all about that worry until right this moment. My mind cleared. I looked at the agent, waiting for his next move.

He cleared his throat. "When did you enter Turkey?"

I had nothing else to say. I looked at him, defeated.

We stared at each other. My look was not a hostile look, it was closer to resignation, as if admitting that whatever happened next was up to him; I'd already played my only card.

His eyes darted from my passport to my face. After a time he prompted, "You went to Kaş ..."

I stared at him, wondering what Kaş had to do with me entering the country, and then I remembered.

"Oh. Right." I exhaled, quickly. "I went to Greece for a day, which was out of the country, then I reentered at the end of the day...I took a ferry from Kaş, I think it was July 10th or so?"

He nodded, handed me my passport and sent me forward in the line.

I had a few minutes to catch my breath before the next stop.

Every one of us in the line had to go through a third security check. "Where are you from? Where are you going now? How many days were you in Turkey?"

I'd gotten used to seeing security guards in all public places around the country, holding machine guns where one hand holds the trigger area and the other hand holds the top of the gun, pointed down. I'd gotten used to passing through a security x-ray machine for every museum, bus station and airport I visited, but I'd never expected it would take so long to get to my departure gate. Good thing I arrived at the airport early.

The American woman in front of me, who was about my age, stood with her arms folded over her chest and demanded, "Why must I?" as if she'd reached her personal limit when it came to answering questions. To repay her for her question, they spent extra time searching her.

I agreed with her, there may have been a few questions more than necessary, but I hid my annoyance.

There were more stops to make. My carry-on bag had to be hand-searched. A security guard unpacked every trinket from my bag and piled them between us on a table. She felt around all the edges to be sure there wasn't something else hidden along a seam.

Another security agent approached me and said, in English, something I couldn't understand.

"Sorry?" I said. "What did you say?"

"Lady," she said, and then said some other words.

Had I done something wrong? I shook my head slowly to show I didn't understand.

She said it again, "Lady..."

I checked my ankle, thinking I was bleeding again, darn ankle. I had crushed the back of my right sneaker under my foot, making my shoe a slide-on and wore two socks on that foot to hold the injury together. My friend, Rich, was going to pick me up in the airport in New York City; I wasn't sure if my ankle could stand a lot of walking and I hoped it wouldn't start bleeding again.

I listened intently and figured out that the agent wanted me to take off my shoes for a security screening.

She dabbed my hair, my clothes, and the inside of my shoes with a tag, then put them into a machine.

There was only one more table in the long line of screenings. A woman stepped forward to pat me down. I stood calmly with my arms out to the sides as she passed her monitor over my body.

I left this last search and handed my passport to one last agent, the Agent at the End of the Line.

He said, "Did you like Turkey?"

This was not a typical question and so I had to dig a little deeper past my memorized answers: "July 3rd, Izmir, Kingston, New York, Turkish Airlines."

I smiled. "Yes. I liked Turkey very much."

He narrowed his gaze. "Tell me one thing you learned."

I raised my eyebrows. "I like Turkish delight."

He laughed and told me that I had good taste and handed back my passport.

As I walked towards the gate area, I looked back at the angry American woman who was still arguing as they searched her bag, again. Did she have something illegal in there? The security agents wondered too. Now there was another guard standing next to her; this one had a machine gun.

"She is with you? She is you family?" the agent who had just released me asked.

Note to self: Never show curiosity at an airport. Never. Ever.

"No," I said, looking at him. "I am alone. My people are quieter."

He laughed and permitted me to pass.

The gate area was quarantined from all other gate areas by large, thick plastic walls.

Time to go home.

Home.

My friend Liz, her sister and her sister's children stayed in my house while I was away and watered my plants. The children sent me a sweet video thanking me for letting them stay in my house, and let me know that they found the hidden toy chest and that they were really glad I mentioned it, because they never would have found it without my note.

I had a little contract with my sister, Heather. She insisted I send her text messages about where I was staying every night, but failed to notice when my phone stopped working and the texts stopped coming in.

Six months after I was home, a text would arrive on her phone. "I'll be at the beach in Çirali for the next three nights. Can't wait to get some ocean time!" The text confused us both. Where had that message been hiding?

My time in Turkey was over.

I went to a snack bar in my gate area and bought three bottles of water, which cost as much as bottles of water would cost at an airport in New York. I thought this was a great bargain when the only alternative would be to go back into the main airport to buy water, and then return to my gate area and go through those screenings again.

No thanks.

As I walked onto the plane, I thought about a line from my favorite Turkish poet, Aurum Ventura: "When you leave, keep the door open."

Home. It was time to go home.

The moment I walked onto the plane was the moment my travel story ended.

Rather than fall into a depression, I watched the other passengers. Most of them were Turkish. They carried large parcels filled with food from the airport to make the flight tastier.

This truly was the end.

Though I'd paid Turkish Airlines extra money to secure a window seat on the way to Turkey and on the way home, I was given a middle seat for both flights.

That's okay. I can sit anywhere.

The next time you see me, you might ask me about my Turkish summer. If you do, I will smile the small smile of remembering and will condense this glorious adventure into three small words:

It was good.

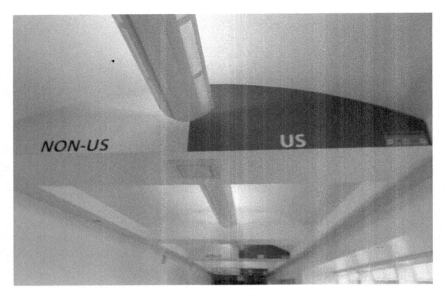

Customs in the USA.

Holly Winter Huppert stands in the front yard of her house where the
weeds have grown over her head

EPILOGUE: CHEESE FOR BREAKFAST

My friend Rich picked me up at the airport in New York City. As soon as I was settled into his car, he said, "How was it?"

I mentally arranged stories in my head, ready to regale him with as many things as I could for the two-hour ride home, but was so exhausted from the time difference that I fell asleep and slept most of the way home.

He woke me when we arrived at my house. "I hope you didn't sleep through all of Turkey."

I've been home several days now and had time to unpack, buy groceries and had a long phone call with my mother. Between the jet lag and mixed-up time zones, I was hungry for breakfast at 2:00 AM, but made myself wait until 5:30 AM, just before sunrise.

With the artist sleeping next to me, I snuck out of bed, closed the bedroom door behind me and went to the kitchen to forage for breakfast. Normally I chose between oatmeal, an egg wrap or a smoothie for breakfast. What did I want to eat this morning?

Cheese.

I opened the white sheep's cheese I'd ordered on the internet and placed a wedge in a bowl, then dug around the refrigerator for what I might add. Olives. A hardboiled egg. Cut-up pieces of tomato and cucumber. A slice of watermelon. It was the same breakfast I'd had almost every day all summer.

I carried the food down the three flights of stairs to my dock and watched the wildlife around the creek become more active as the sun rose. Birds sang as they flew over my head. Ducks paddled past me on their way to somewhere else. A squirrel jumped from a small tree to a larger tree, as if refusing to touch the ground. I studied the trees' reflections in the water until I could imagine another world, right there, under the surface.

It was quiet on the dock. So very quiet. Later tonight my girl group would bring me dinner, and we would kayak and roast marshmallows in the fire pit the artist put together for me, and I'd tell them stories about my summer away and gift them with small amulets of the evil eye so that they might keep bad luck at bay.

I ate slowly, with my hands, feeling lucky that I had all the ingredients for a proper Turkish breakfast.

I saved the cheese for last, as I always do. There's nothing like cheese for breakfast, but it's doubly good to eat cheese for breakfast's dessert.

Zing. There was a bit of a zing in the cheese.

I furrowed my brow and tried another piece. What was that zing?

Spoiled. The cheese had gone bad. So much for ordering specialty cheese on the internet.

The beauty around me diminished. Rotten cheese for breakfast?

I tried to laugh it off but was offended; that cheese was expensive.

Maybe it was time to release my hold on Turkey. My travels were over. It was time to fully return home, where I had many blessings.

In two weeks, the artist and I would travel to New York City so I could fit a bit more adventure into my summer while he had some work to do there.

I took a deep breath and absorbed the beauty around me. "I'm so lucky to live here," I said out loud, for the thousandth time since I bought this property.

I climbed back up to the house, dropped my dishes in the sink and made my way to the artist, still asleep in my bed.

Yes. I had many blessings.

Acknowledgments

A big thank you to Hunker Keser, the archaeologist, and your amazing family: your beautiful wife Zehara and your smart-thoughtful-talented daughter Karya for hosting me, taking me on the best picnics of my life, sharing your friends, directing photoshoots and talking me through every site and museum in your area. When you suggested I cook one meal for you, I got a little tense; your cooking is so much better. I promise, if you come to visit me one day in upstate New York you can cook for me here, too. Bring cheese. And tomatoes. And olives. And that lamb stew you made the first night. And that red breakfast paste. I love you all and look forward to seeing you again. We are family now.

Thank you to the English teacher Menekşe, your husband Talat, and your beautiful smart, caring, funny long-haired daughter Azra for the time we spent together in Selçuk. I appreciate you answering every one of my questions, explaining the dress code and teaching me about the history of Turkey. I will always remember the tomato joke. I look forward to seeing you again, my dear friends.

Thank you to the librarian Emine and your sister Şerife for hosting me in Atabey, showing me small-town life and sharing your extended family with me. Your father is a true gem and I loved playing cards with your children. If you were not so far away, I would meet you at the lilac farm for a cup of tea every afternoon. I hope your library grows; it is such a beautiful project. I will think of both of you every time I see ducks swimming in a row. We will be friends forever; of this I am sure.

Thank you to Mehmet, my friend in Konya for taking me on a tour to the archaeological site, to visit the nomads, the barbecue at the top of the mountain and to your family's village, and for patiently answering my questions about nomads. I am unsure which part of our day I will treasure the most, your story or our adventures. Perhaps they are both equal. One day I will return. I will.

Thank you to the eight-year-old girl on the bus who was forced to sit next to me, even though your mother protested. I think of you often and the way you insisted that the attendant give me a drink; you refused to back down until he did: such courage from one so young. You stood up to a cruel man on my behalf; I bow to your bravery and thank you for your kindness.

Thank you to my mother for being my biggest encourager in all I do. Thanks to my sister Heather for trying to keep track of where I was—in case I went missing. Thanks to my brother, Darius for checking in with me when I was on the road.

Thanks to Sonia, a friend who is always ready to help me celebrate a new journey and then hear the stories after. Thanks, Amy and Tim, for making sure my travel addiction was nurtured. Thanks to Liz for taking care of my house while I was away; my plants love you. Thanks, Rich, for the airport shuttle service.

And to my neighbor Tara who left a care package with treats on my front doorstep so I had food in the house after being away for six weeks. I. Was. So. Hungry. Thank you.

Thank you to my forever friend, Lynda, for laughing at my travel habit, and then insisting on hearing every story as soon as I returned and then gifting me with a new computer to finish this book. I am lucky to have you in my corner.

I offer big love for my girl group, The Normals (Gayle, Julie, Linda, Anne, Marge, Diane, Heather and Bonnie), who celebrated my sendoff with a party, and then welcomed me home with another party. I value our friendships and cherish our time together. Thanks for making everything fun.

To Betsy Osgood, my editor of many years, thank you. Your golden touch makes everything I write better-er. I am deeply grateful to have you on my team.

And big gratitude to the friends on my website and on Facebook who read and celebrated my journey with me. Thank you for the ongoing encouragement.

And you, dear reader. Thank you for buying this book and supporting small publishers. Thank you from the bottom of my heart for supporting this book. If you loved *Cheese for Breakfast*, please consider leaving a review on your social media sites and buying a copy for a deserving friend.

Thank you to the many people in my life who understand me. At my very core, I am one who is at home anywhere in the world; I am a traveler.

About Holly Winter Huppert

Holly Winter Huppert is a writer, a photographer and a teacher who travels from upstate New York where she lives. Here she photographs a mosaic in the Terrace House exhibit of Ephesus.

Connect with Holly Winter Huppert:
Instagram @ mshollywinter
Facebook @ mshollywinter
Website: www.hollywinter.com

~

Find her latest books on winuplypress.com including **Write Now: Ideas for Writers** which is a book of writing prompts for children.

~

Hans Helps: A Coronavirus/COVID-19 Story tells of a boy who learns how to protect his extended family from the coronavirus.

~

Unlikely Memories and Two Amnesias is her memoir published under the name, "Holly Winter."

Next:

The hardcover coffee table book, ***Turkish Summer: Photos from Cheese for Breakfast***, is now available in color everywhere books are sold.

⮑

For Holly Winter Huppert's video that complements the book, go to YouTube and search for ***Cheese for Breakfast: My Turkish Summer***.

⮑

Ready for another travel book by Holly Winter Huppert? ***No Ketchup in Cuba?*** is due the fall of 2021. Go to www.winuplypress.com to sign up for email alerts.

⮑

Dear Reader, please write a review of this book at winuplypress.com and on your social media sites. Thank you for supporting small publishers.

⮑

Winuply Press
Books for All

Please send your friends and family to www.winuplypress.com or anywhere books are sold to buy additional copies of ***Cheese for Breakfast: My Turkish Summer*** and to get the companion book: ***Turkish Summer: Photos from Cheese for Breakfast***.